SIX WOMEN POETS

A CROSS-CULTURAL STUDY

Emily Dickinson | Sarojini Naidu
Sylvia Plath | Kamala Das Surayya
Adrienne Rich | Mamta Kalia

MINA SURJIT SINGH

PRESTIGE

Published by

Prestige Books
3/28, East Patel Nagar
New Delhi 110 008

ISBN: 81-7551-143-5

Printed at Chaman Offset Press, New Delhi 110 002

Contents

To my husband Saru

Acknowledgements

I must express my gratitude to my family for bearing with me throughout the period of my engagement with this study. Without their support and involvement, this book would not have been possible. Special thanks are due to the Panjab University, Chandigarh, for granting me two years' sabbatical to pursue work on my proposal; to Dr. R.K. Dhawan for helping in its publication and to Sarabjit and R.P. Aggarwal for providing valuable assistance in typing the manuscript.

The bulk of reading material for this project was provided by the A.C. Joshi Library, Panjab University, Chandigarh, the Indo-American Centre for International Studies, Hyderabad (erstwhile *ASRC*), the British Council and the American Centre Libraries, New Delhi and the Indian Institute for Advanced Studies, Shimla, for which I am grateful.

Poetry is not a luxury.

Audre Lorde

Introduction

> To write is a solitary and singular act; to do it superbly . . . is a blessing. Despite everything that gets said about the suffering and panic and horror of being a writer, the final impression . . . is one of thankfulness, of humility in the face of what has been given.
>
> Margaret Atwood

Feminist scholarship has provided some of the most enduring and comprehensive frameworks for understanding the patriarchal nature of the modern state. Women's movements and writings have certainly made women more cognizant of their own inequality and have brought to public attention the violence and indignity, which has informed women's dependent status within family and society. Focusing on the many subtle ways in which the lived experiences of women have been sieved out as extraneous, irrelevant and sometimes even anomalous to a sanitized account of history, women's writings have prized open the complexities which are shrouded in universalistic histories, wherein oppressive practices have been silenced. Public policies and plan perspectives relating to women's issues reflect and reinforce an ideology, which locates women's agencies firmly within national, religious and cultural boundaries. Further, circumscribed by the boundaries of community, women are received as members of society on the basis of their socially useful role as mothers, which is considered women's supreme function in life, thereby submerging them in an inviolable biological determinism. In a recent book *Backlash: The Undeclared War against American Women*, Susan Faludi, the Pulitzer Prize-winning newspaper reporter, has documented through statistical evidence, how media-generated images of women have contributed towards major setbacks to the women's movements every time they have made modest gains toward gender equality. Defining the backlash as a powerful counter-assault on women's autonomy and rights, which is at once "sophisticated and banal, deceptively 'progressive' and proudly 'backward,'" she enlists several strategies through which, it has succeeded in "framing the whole issue of women's rights in its own language." (467) The backlash, which Faludi attributes to male anxiety over women's equality, pursues a "divide-and-conquer" strategy by working subliminally to recruit women against their own cause and has even succeeded in convincing the public that women have been enslaved by their own liberation. We are told time and again that the women's movement has proved woman's greatest enemy. By "deploying both 'new' findings of 'scientific research' and the dime-store moralism of yesteryear," (462) the backlash is a "preemptive strike" to push women back into more acceptable roles as home-makers and passive love objects even before they "reach the finish line." (464) This strengthens the grounds for a gendered citizenship governed by the complex web of religious sanction, social taboos and cultural conventions. Two key concepts that provide a framework for the analysis of power and the manner in which it unfolds in ruling practices creating deeply entrenched hierarchies, are 'gender' or sexual difference and 'patriarchy' defined by Adrienne Rich as "the power of the father." Notions of equality and justice get enmeshed in the intricate web of these hierarchies having wide ramifications for what it means to be a woman.

If we were to study women's writing from the point of view of 'feminist style' we would notice several recurring traits and arrive at several conclusions about the female mind and the peculiar tension between the public and private reality that underwrites women's writing. As women's experience is different from men's, they write not only out of that difference, that is their feminine consciousness, but also out of their difference of view and standard in a social order in which they are 'alien,' 'other' or marginal, to the standard referent. Commenting on the work of women poets, Wendy Martin cogently suggests: "Traditionally women's history and literature have not been monumental in scope and do not lend themselves to heroic declamation . . . [which] requires a command of public space that women have not had. The images of women's experience come more from daily life. . . . Because these women poets reject the hierarchies that accord more importance to public than to private life, their poetry is not a narrative of sublime moments but a chronicle of the quotidian." (10)

Women critics have been particularly concerned with focusing on just where lies that difference. The rift experienced by women writers in a patriarchal society, where "language itself may re-inscribe the structure by which they are oppressed" (Jacobus 10), is also uncovered by some recurring narrative strategies that are discernible and demonstrable in women's writing. Women's writing very often transgresses the boundaries laid down by a patriarchal ideology that inscribes the notion of "virgin, wife, mother" (Jacobus 10), on to women. This comes to represent everything a woman is 'supposed' to be—sympathetic, charming, utterly unselfish, domestic, self-sacrificing and above all, *pure*, even if the nature is factitious. For, as Jane Flax says, "our upbringing . . . often encourages us to deny the many subtle forms of aggression that intimate relations with others can evoke and entail. . . . Perhaps women are not any less aggressive than men; we may just express our aggression in different, culturally sanctioned (and partially disguised or denied) ways." (55) The tradition of women's writing thus becomes an "exit from the sacred to the profane." (Jacobus 10) Innocent, angelic and nubile creatures miraculously metamorphose into 'sinful' adventuresses. In the course of fulfilling their desires as writers, they are forced to hurt or fail those they love most and bring upon themselves anxiety, unhappiness, loneliness, alienation, solipsism and public censure, for having silenced the 'feminine' and sacrificed their ancient consciousness of silent suffering. But in Paula Bennett's pithy formulation: "People not angels create art." (10) In their attempts to transcend the imprisoning patriarchal determinants of gender and culture, these writers no longer suffer in silence but seek to educate themselves about their own true natures/selves, as well as about the lies that have been foisted on them, through centuries of historic distortions and control. Since experience forms the basis of female creativity, it is important for women writers to realize that the self, whatever that self may be, is the basis upon which they must work, for it alone can be the source of their greatest authority and strength.

While eschewing prescriptions on what and how to write, there is almost a conspiratorial tendency in women's writings, to overthrow all the pleasing, agreeable patterns and associations of a male tradition. This tradition has treated writing primarily as a male preserve and men's writings as though it were a model for all writing. Even though there may be some common ground between the writing of men and women and their language may reflect this similarity, there is bound to be a difference in representation because the setting for both is different. Any criticism of a literary text from a political or feminist perspective then, allows us to better define the portrayal of attitudes towards women. It also allows an exposure of the ways in which stereotyped formulations of women's roles in society and the reproduction of sexist ideology by male critics get codified in literary texts. The major assumption behind this kind of criticism is that stereotypical portrayals of women are politically interested figurations and tropes that pass off as truth and that there is something unique about women's writing, which gains special significance as a practical way of influencing everyday conduct, attitudes and mindset. It is a form of affirmative action against oppressive forces that systematically marginalize women to disadvantageous positions. Self-assertion in women's writing, then, is seen not only as a form of resistance against basic power relations between men and women, but also as a challenge to patriarchy as the primeval source of power and to the existing social structures that perpetuate the exploitation and subjugation of women. Women's writings, thus, emerge as a site for negotiations of progressive political readings, in their attempt to relocate women in the social structure.

As a society alters its definition of what is appropriate, it also alters its notions of how artists may express themselves, though the commonly accepted rules of discourse might be different for men and women. These norms in turn determine the parameters of what may or may not be expressed, revealed or even admitted as true or meaningful. However, what is taken as the 'norm' is never neutral or universal but governed by the specific 'requirements' of a class or society. As such, what women have so far expressed is what they have been able to express. Annette Kolodony, the feminist critic, lays great emphasis on the significant influence of biology and acculturation on expression and perception. In her essay, 'Some Notes on Defining a "Feminist Literary Criticism",' she draws attention to, "the complex interplay of innate biological determinants, personal and individual talents and opportunities and the larger effects of socialization, which . . . govern the limits of expression or even perception and experience itself." (76) She argues further, that in literature particularly, "this gets translated into an interplay between inherited tradition and conscious artistic choice" (77), resulting in what may sometimes seem eccentric, bizarre or even exaggerated perceptions of reality. Nonetheless, this artistic choice must neither be slighted nor dismissed as it often is, as the manifestation of neurosis or sensationalistic motives when we study the use women make of language in the process of self-discovery. Images of women writers as 'lightweight puff balls, neurotic freaks suffering from . . . "a double dose of masochism, the masochism of the woman and that of the artist"' (Atwood XIV), abound in male criticism of women's texts, thus contributing to their systematic devaluation through injudicious masculinist interpretations. Joyce Carol Oates too, speaks for women writers in general, when she says that she has often had to face the difficulty of not being "*taken altogether* seriously *by the sort of male critics who rank writers 1,2,3 in the public press.*" (qtd. Atwood XIII) This point finds suitable illustration in Ezra Pound's disparaging comment on women writers, wherein he says: "I distrust the 'female artist.' . . . Not wildly anti-feminist we are yet to be convinced that any woman ever invented anything in the arts." (qtd. Atwood XIV) It is in this context, that the concept of silence and silencing becomes central to the discussion of women's participation in the production of literary culture. Atwood reiterates that this prejudice of the male critic has been operative before and ever since, bringing into sharp focus the relatedness of poetry and patriarchy. As such, male scholarship on women's texts needs to be looked upon with suspicion for its tendencies to dismiss women writers through clichés. Women's writings need to be revealed and re-evaluated through a fair and unbiased appraisal, which can only be possible if a sincere attempt is made to understand the many layers of female experience and its consequent verbal expression. As Elaine Showalter, a feminist critic and Professor of English at Princeton says, recent feminist criticism has therefore, shifted from "revisionary readings to a sustained investigation of literature by women." (335) This kind of woman-centered critical discourse, which she terms as 'gynocritics,' engenders the "study of women as *writers*," or in other words, an investigation into "the psychodynamics of female creativity." (335) Showalter is suspicious of 'feminist critique' because of its reliance on theory, which she characterizes as masculine and because it teaches women to read like men and gloss over the difference of female experience. On the other hand, gynocritical modes of reading would reflect the real situation of women, would dig into myth-making tradition and articulate for them the unsaid, the muffled, and the silent.

Generally the female writer is seen as suffering the handicap of having to work within the framework of the dominant discourse, which Adrienne Rich calls "the oppressor's language," in the absence of a form of language that is inherently feminine. This assumption is based on Dale Spender's thesis in *Man Made*

Language, in which she argues that women have been marginalized by patriarchal structures of language and knowledge. Her contention is that language, a supposedly gender-neutral structure, both names and produces superiority (for example, in the use of a masculine universal pronoun and in words such as 'chairman' and 'master'). Language, she argues, is masculine and "not a neutral medium but one which contains many features which reflect its role as the instrument through which patriarchy finds expression." (qtd. Barry 127) In the absence of neutral norms and neutral language, women's writing turns solipsistic so that, even while necessarily working within the dominant culture and discourse, it seeks "ceaselessly to deconstruct it: to write what cannot be written." (Jacobus 13) It attempts to speak not only against, but also outside the phallocentric structure and to evolve a language that is not oppressive, a language that "does not render speechless but loosens the tongue." (Showalter 339) In this context, Adrienne Rich, the American feminist poet-critic, believes that:

> A radical critique of literature, feminist in its impulse, would take the work first of all as a clue to how we live, how we have been living, how we have been led to imagine ourselves, how our language has trapped as well as liberated us, how the very act of naming has been till now a male prerogative, and how we can begin to see and name—and therefore live—afresh. (35).

Women's writing thus, has the political agenda of abrogating and appropriating the patriarchal ideology that inscribes women's marginality. This agenda is articulated as a double-voiced discourse which "embodies the social, literary and cultural heritages of both the muted and the dominant" (Showalter 348) and therefore contains a dominant, as well as a muted story. While it could declare overt and strident warfare against patriarchy on the one hand, it could also engage in guerilla tactics through the subversive strategies of reticence, irony, understatement and indirection on the other, in its attempt to vitiate dominant patriarchal and sexist assumptions. One can, therefore, perceive clearly demonstrable repetitions of particular thematic concerns, image patterns and stylistic devices in such gender-polarized writings and interpretations. Although male writers share many of these as well, they are without central emphasis on the peculiarly feminine positional connotations they hold in women's writing.

At the close of the twentieth century, much of women's writings are about questioning identity—a single identity of birth, country, community. Often it is about exploring the ambiguities of a dual identity, a divided self and a growing awareness of other cultures, other sensibilities across the world, which gives them the freedom to question their own worldview. Women live in duality, that is as members of a general culture or dominant group, which is androcentric and as partakers of a women's culture, which constitutes the muted group whose realities and culture are not contained by the dominant group. This concept of women's culture incorporates ideas of a distinct female *`ecriture* that is style, tone, language, feeling about women, their bodies, their psyche, but interprets them in the social context in which they occur. It defines women's activities from a 'woman-centered' point of view, which consciously focuses on women and addresses the distinctiveness of. female experience implying, both "an assertion of equality and an awareness of sisterhood, the community of women." (Showalter 345-46) Even while taking cognizance of the difference between races, class, nationality, history, ethnic groups and other subjective variables, it binds women together in a larger context over time and space. Their idea of female bonding, which is different from the Marxian concept of cultural hegemony, is seen as the strength of cultural feminism, which makes a plea for women's culture. This culture is not to be treated as a sub-culture but is to be recognized for its strengths and capabilities. Although female bonding may be scorned and scoffed at in general, it may be the invisible means of strengthening in virtue. As Showalter points out: "One of the greatest advantages of the woman's-culture mode is that it shows how the female tradition can be a positive source of strength and solidarity as well as negative source of powerlessness; it can generate its own experiences and symbols which are not simply the obverse of the male tradition." (350) It is the conviction of cultural feminists that societies suffer because women are not given their due rights and place. Women's culture recognizes the collective experience of women within a larger cultural context and claims full autonomy from patriarchal institutions, which encourage sex-role socialization and relegate women to second position. It is this phenomenon of inferiorisation that spurs a woman's struggle for self-definition.

In the struggle for freedom from all forms of oppression—familial, social, political, institutional—in which, by force or customs, etiquette, education or even division of labor, the female is subsumed by the male, the woman writer embarks on a personal odyssey. This journey to the dark continent visualized as "the mother country of liberated desires and female authenticity" (Showalter 347), is undertaken in order to release and realize the full potential of her complex identity as a woman and as a writer. A prototypical journey that derives its consciousness from the group experience of women, it begins in physical and psychological bondage and envisions a new world of mutual respect and justice as its end. Through a voluntary entry into the consciousness of the female, women hope to write their way out of the cramped confines of patriarchal space. Much of the vitality of women's writing derives from an attempt to subvert the conventional and stereotypical image of womanhood as passive, self-sacrificing and contented that ignores the wide-ranging efforts and achievements of scores of outstanding women. Through the very act of subversion, it reflects a new awareness of culture-specific power relations that contribute towards divisive polarities. In attempting to capture authentically, the nitty-gritty of women's lives—the reality we must address ourselves to—women writers reassert the authority of subjective experience. Their writing is no longer an engagement with maudlin autobiography but a brave and courageous act, which is poetic and political, passionate and objective even while drawing on passionate and objective even while drawing on subjective experience.

Poetry can never be read as if it had not been written by anybody in particular. It is always the product of the person. The relationship between art and biography is an exigency of feminist criticism and most scholars of the genre do recognize the constant speculation between self-representation and art. So also, there is an ideological link between the lives and art of the poets this study concerns itself with, which is informed by their need for gender identification and liberation from the stifling patriarchal culture of their historical realities. The work of these writers is about inherent strength and control, about empowerment through a recognition and release of this strength and through emotional and intellectual assertions that challenge existing power relationships, by extolling the virtues of sharing and caring. The empirical psychologist Carol Gilligan could very well be speaking for them when she says:

> As we have listened for centuries to the voices of men . . . so we have come more recently to notice not only the silence of women but the difficulty in hearing what they say when they speak. Yet in the different voice of women lies the truth of an ethic of care. (173)

The poetry of these women then, articulates their attempts to build a positive structure on the negative foundation they have inherited, even as they envision new human and communal possibilities. By upholding the nurturing ethos of the feminine, these writers seek to transform the existing power structure into an alternate structure in which, as Rich says:

> Power instead of a thing to be hoarded by few, would be released to and from within the many, shared in the form of knowledge, expertise, decision making. (*BBP* 5)

In powerful patriarchies, that is men and the structures of domination they have made, these voices have in their own way, made significant contributions towards a female bonding. This would not only help women to understand themselves and other women, but also help men to understand them better since, both men and women are mutually engaged in the important business of living balanced and meaningful lives. For, even though cultural feminists are concerned with woman and womanhood: "oppressed and devalued by, but also standing in opposition to the patriarchy," (Evans 93) cultural feminism is heterogeneous. It is undoubtedly a sex or gender difference school but not necessarily a "celebrator of difference." (Evans 88) Its concerns are humanitarian. The individual experiences of these poets have their validity in the universal context of collective womanhood so that localized identities of race, color and nationality are ultimately subsumed in that collectivity. Their writings lend voice to the scores of women whose voices have been silenced or remained unheard. They speak for the scores of 'Mary Anns' (to borrow the name from the telling title of Australian woman writer Beverley Kingston's book, *My Wife, My Daughter, Poor Mary Ann*), whose identities have been submerged and achievements undermined by patriarchy. Their poetry, in the broader context of women's experience in diverse cultures, illustrates how the work of significant artists helps to explain their era and our own. For the most part, there are many rewards in the approach and method of these writers for the attentive reader, in terms of insight and overview. If the western woman's psyche is overtaken by anger and rage, the Indian woman poet's psyche is dominated by a sense of disappointment and longing for the ideal. The overwhelming concern of all these writers, however, is to subvert the role of 'true' womanhood as laid down and understood in diverse historical and cultural contexts. Their attempt is to explore the common experiences of women that transcend national boundaries, for only women can describe and say what women are and how they are to be valued. As Schneir rightly states, woman alone can understand "the height, the depth, the length and the breadth of her own degradation." (ix) In this context, these women poets can be placed in the tradition of cultural feminist, whose major concern is with the redress of women and all those who have been wrongly depicted by men. As Linda Alcoff says: "[Construing] women's passivity as her peacefulness, her sentimentality as her proclivity to nurture, her subjectiveness as her advanced self-awareness. . . . Cultural feminists have not challenged the defining of woman but only that definition given by men." (297)

These women seek empowerment, which for them may flow from within or without. Perceived as an inherent strength, it may manifest itself in several ways, in so much as it enables them to make choices and live their lives on their own terms, even while playing a significant role in social reconstruction. Their attempts to express themselves as women within their culture specifics and the larger global culture in particular, need to be appreciated and highlighted. These poets see their art as an act of resistance and a source of inherent power and energy. They then show us through their art the ways in which small acts of resistance that people perform can help change lives and perceptions.

The intention in this study is not to provide a comprehensive account of Indian and American women's poetry but to bring together six temperaments. It examines the work of six representative poets against the backdrop of their historical time and space, in order to understand how their experience as women and poets, has been the focus of their poetic concerns and poetic vision. These poets have experienced fear and pain along with their growth as writers and women and possess the ability to speak for and interpret the truths of their sex. This study has been undertaken in the conviction that Sarojini Naidu, Kamala Das and Mamta Kalia have a special place in the history of twentieth century women's poetry in India, just as Emily Dickinson, Sylvia Plath and Adrienne Rich are significant contributors to the tradition of women's poetry in America. Their role has grown not only because of the expanding expectations of their community, but also because of the expectations of the growing congregation of women writers in general. Their work reflects diversity and provides a sample of some fine writings by women in the twc countries. Their narrative traces the desire for freedom from gender oppression, from its abstract underpinnings to its concrete manifestation, even while it examines the construction of female identity through mythicised conceptions of women. More importantly, it is bound together by the framework of a common concern and engagement with communal obligation. In its commitment towards building and renewing a sense of collective life, their work records a movement from spectatorial detachment, to the predicament of unscrolling a map on which gender intersects in a shared landscape. Their shared project is to bring into being, the symbolic weight of women's consciousness to make the invisible visible, to make the silent speak. Brought up with all the visible trappings of emancipated women with a covert traditional agenda, these women were encouraged to work and be independent but also to get married and have children. Straddling two worlds, one representing tradition the other modernity, one freedom the other bondage, one progression the other regression, these women have braved the perils of the tight-rope-walker and emerged triumphant. The women included in this study have a special kind of complexity. They are concerned with the overlapping worlds of tradition and skepticism, of collective responsibility and individual choice and with striking a tenuous balance. While working within the tradition of social comment, they have added different dimensions by bringing new material into their poetry with their strong portraits of women. The attempt is to move away from the notion of women as figures of exploitation and victimization and to look instead, for a more complimentary and challenging representation of women through different local experiences and traditions. With a remarkable sense of honesty and conviction, these women have helped establish an entirely new poetic, a new way for women to recreate themselves in art as figures of power, in their passionate concern for women and for a more humane society. In writing then, these women are writing a New World.

Works Cited

Alcoff, Linda. "Cultural feminism versus post-structuralism: the identity crisis in feminist theory." *Feminist Theory in Practice and Process*. Ed. Micheline R. Malson et al. Chicago and London: University of Chicago Press. 1989. 295-32

Atwood, Margaret. "Introduction." *The Paris Review Interviews: Women Writers at Work*. Ed. George Plimpton. London: The Harvile Press. 1999. VIII-XVIII.

Barry, Peter. 1995. *Beginning Theory*. Manchester: University Press.

Bennett, Paula. 1986. *My Life A Loaded Gun: Female Creativity and Feminist Poetics*. Boston: Beacon Press.

Evans, Judith. 1996. *Feminist Theory Today: An Introduction to Second-Wave Feminism*. London: Sage Publications.

Flax, Jane. "Postmodernism and gender relations in feminist theory." *Feminism/ Postmodernism*. Ed. Linda Nicholson. London: Routledge 1990. 39-62.

Gilligan, Carol. 1992. *In a Different Voice*. London: Harvard University Press.

Jacobus, Mary. 1979. "The Difference of View." *Women Writing and Writing about Women*. Ed. Jacobus. New York: Barnes and Noble. Imports.

Kolodny, Annette. 'Some Notes on Defining a "Feminist Literary Criticism."' *Critical Inquiry*. 2. Autumn 1975. 75-92.

Rich, Adrienne. 1979. *On Lies, Secrets and Silences: Selected Prose 1966-1978*. New York: W.W. Norton.

______. 1986. *Blood, Bread and Poetry: Selected Prose 1979-1985*. New York: W.W. Norton. (Hereafter cited as *BBP*).

Schneir, Miriam. Ed. 1995. *The Vintage Book of Feminism*. New York: Vintage Books

Showalter, Elaine. "Feminist Criticism in the Wilderness." *Modern Criticism and Theory*. Ed. David Lodge. London and New York: Longman. 1988. 331-53.

Spender, Dale. 1985. *Man Made Language*. London: Routledge and Kegan Pa

Genius in the Wilderness: Emily Dickinson

The grace—Myself—might not obtain—
Confer upon My flower—
Refracted but a Countenance—
For I—inhabit Her—

Emily Dickinson

The significant ways in which the poetry Emily Dickinson, one of the greatest women poets and one of the greatest poets in the history of American literature, has contributed to the evolution of an ever-expanding female literary tradition can never be over-emphasized. Not only has her poetry retained its enigmatic force through decades of attempts to explain and contain it, but it has also provided a means for developing more penetrating and ingenious readings of the verse of other women, both within and beyond her century. As Karl Keller suggests: "Emily Dickinson, more than most writing women . . . before the mid-twentieth century, convinces one that the female is more than a gender, more in fact a separate species." (Keller 68) Her work is of especial value because, at a time when woman and poet were treated as mutually exclusive terms, Dickinson uses her femaleness to challenge restrictive and debilitating hierarchical structures to create a poetic identity that would affect a conjunction between biography and poetry, woman and poet. She can, then, be seen as the harbinger of a self-empowering world in which one can "find ecstasy in living." [*L* viii]

Emily Dickinson was born in 1830 to a family well known for educational and political activity, in the midst of a rigid Puritanical community, and lived out the entire drama of her life at # 280 Main Street, Amherst, Western Massachusetts. Paradoxically enough, this New England community, which insisted on demarcating and defining clearly the religious and socially acceptable ways in which men and women were expected to live out their lives, was to become the greatest source of her empowerment. No poet has, probably ever, lived so much and so purposefully in one house; rather, in one room, that is, her bedroom on the second floor of the house. This was to become her retreat and refuge from the pressures of the outside world and it was here, as she confessed to her niece Martha Bianchi, that she had found her freedom. The power and effect of her Puritan heritage as well as the country that was witness to religious revivals, spiritual confrontations and evangelical passions, can be undeniably felt within her work and as Dickinson herself admitted, she saw "New Englandly." In May 1850, she wrote to Abiah Root, the closest of her once inseparable circle of five school friends. Her letter acknowledged her growing sense of alienation and rebellion against the fate to which she was assigned by: "the laws of God, made known by nature and by providence and also by the Bible." (Bennett 17) These laws demanded that she take up the conventional duties of a woman as embodied in the evangelical doctrine of usefulness or doing good for others in imitation of Christ, whether these duties fitted her gifts or not. During this time, Dickinson had been confined to household chores, as also, to nursing her ailing mother suffering from "Acute Neuralgia" (*L* 38) and the heavily sardonic tone of her letter is unmistakably expressive of her sense of rage and entrapment:

> I am yet the Queen of the Court, if regalia be dust and dirt, have three loyal subjects, whom I'd rather relieve from service. Mother is still an invalid tho' a partially restored one—Father and Austin still clamor for food, and I, like a martyr am feeding them. Wouldn't you love to see me in these bonds of great despair, looking around my kitchen and praying for kind deliverance, and declaring by "Omar's beard" I never was in such plight. *My* kitchen I think I called it, God forbid that it was, or shall be my own—God keep me from what they call households, except that bright one of "faith." (*L* 40)

For the evangelical educators of Dickinson's day, the goal of education was expedience and not pleasure and yet she "had been dreaming a golden dream, with eyes all the wide open." (*L* 40) The valorization of domesticity and public service demonstrated how the dominant group exercised its hegemony through religion and the education system. The Bible and Christian doctrine formed the basis for learning in every area. The Amherst Academy and Mount Holyoke Female Seminary, which Dickinson attended, were molded by the principle of utilitarianism and public service, which lay in maturing as wives and mothers. Consequently, the students of institutions were instructed in a utilitarian curriculum designed to help them function efficiently in the domestic and social spheres. The primary aim of women's education was to help them to adapt: "Spiritually and psychologically to a role that was deemed by nature and God's law, service-oriented, domestic and subservient to the male." (Bennett 19) Mary Lyon, the founder and president of Mount Holyoke, mockingly referred to as "Mistress Lyon," (*L* 22) very ardently took upon herself the *altruistic* mission of molding the spiritual and moral lives of her young wards towards the development of "correct ideas of female propriety and sedate deportment." (*L* 21) The young women under her charge were trained and encouraged to practise and appreciate the value of self-denial and self-sacrifice. As a natural consequence of such instruction, then, women were preferentially expected to either become teachers or missionaries. If not, then the next best choice of vocation was marriage and motherhood. Thus, the adult life of a middle-class, nineteenth century woman was lived not only in subordination to the male, to society and to religion, but also in willingness to assume her self-sacrificing duties at home and in the world. In desiring a life of pleasure and imagination, then, Dickinson was violating the basic precepts of her time. As Wendy Martin suggests: "In the tradition of protest and reform that is a basic dimension of American culture, she refused to be diminished by the constraints of feminine virtue and propriety that has paralyzed so many Victorian women." (81) Dickinson thus, continued to pursue the solitary and selfish pleasures of her nascent craft, in direct contravention of the requisite subordination of individual proclivities to the welfare of the community. Instead of "doing good," Dickinson chose to court her "dark spirits" and unleash her poetic demons even though it meant behaving in ways that were discordant with her culture's expectations. That she was fully prepared to face the consequences of this disjunction, is quite evident from the letter she wrote to her sister-in-law and confidant Susan Gilbert, with whom she had shared an extremely intimate relationship till the latter's marriage to her brother Austin. In her letter she candidly stated: "though in the last day, the Jesus Christ *you* love, remark he does not know me—there is a darker spirit will not disown its child." (*L* 122) While her friends grew up and endorsed the concept of mature womanhood in the expected manner of wives and mothers, Dickinson chose an unconventional life. She thus became increasingly estranged from the women she was once very close to. In deference to the demands of society and religion, one by one her friends had abandoned her along with their childhood dreams, taking up lives of "usefulness" instead. Joan Bennett informs us that Dickinson's alienation from the friends of her childhood culminated in the early 1850s when Amherst was "swept by waves of evangelical fervor." She goes on to suggest that "conversion" for the young women of that time "was not just an emotional outlet. It was a rite of passage leading them into psychological reconciliation with their adult fates." (26) Dickinson, however, refused to convert and commit herself to narrow sectarianism and spurned thereby a tradition honored by her family for generations. Consequently, no "life choice could have made [her] an anomaly in her society than her desire, however nascent, to be a poet." (Bennett 16) In following her natural propensities, Dickinson's was violating not only the basic prescription of her time, but also the entire thrust of the education she had received at home and at school. Albeit in the process of her struggle to write poetry in an environment that was hostile to the imagination, she was redefining herself not only as a poet but as a woman as well, by subverting the role of the Victorian woman and, more importantly, the tradition of *true* womanhood.

Dickinson's compulsive need for contact with loved ones and more importantly with herself, made her turn to letter-writing which was to become an integral part of her life even while she was still a child. Her earliest surviving letters written when she was only eleven years old and, increasingly so, those written between 1842 and 1846 while she was a young girl on the threshold of adolescence, confirm a charming felicity with words. Besides, these letters form such a rich archive that without them the complete works of Emily Dickinson would not be all that complete. These letters are an invaluable source of information and understanding on crucial phases and aspects of the poet's life. They create an autobiography that chronicles the psychological development of an artist and reveal an acute sensitivity, which marks the incipience of her poetic propensities and her passion for life other than that of gender and cultural compulsions. Apart from this, her letters also shed ample light on Dickinson's family, relatives and friends. Very early in life, Dickinson had expressed her preference for the proscribed life of delight and romance. Her life and art was, thus, committed to the celebration of nature's powers. Her highly excitable nature, her free spirit, her lust for life and the forbidden pleasures of solitude prompted rhapsodic meandering in the woods where Nature's Children: 'might stretch themselves beneath the spreading cypress and close their eyes "calmly as to the night's repose or flowers at set of sun."' (*L* 8) These impulses very naturally then, triggered off an interrogation of the "peculiarly interesting" doctrine of "self-denial" (*L* 8) very early in life. More significantly, these interrogations were initially, often accompanied by a nagging sense of guilt over the pursuit of her innocent desires when she should have been working as enjoined upon by God "while the day last for the night is coming in which no man can work."

(*L* 9) In a letter to Abiah Root in September 1846, Dickinson expressed her fears of impiety and damnation as well as doubts about the validity and acceptability of the Puritan doctrine of salvation through self-denial:

> I feel I have not yet made my peace with God. I am still a s[tran]ger—to the delightful emotions which fill your heart. I have perfect confidence in God and his promise and yet I know not why, I feel that the world holds a predominant place in my affections. I do not feel that I could give up all for Christ, were I called to die. Pray for me dear A. that I may yet enter into the kingdom of heaven, that there may be room left for me in the shining courts above. (*L* 9)

Although Dickinson managed to cope satisfactorily with the studies and a rigorous regimen, the initial enthusiasm of a seventeen-year-old with which she had entered Mount Holyoke was sufficiently dampened. The ideological agenda of moral and social instruction and the heavily charged religious atmosphere of the institution stifled her. Frequently oppressed, she longed to break free of its confines and returned only too happily to "her dear home" at Amherst after a year, even though the move spelt doom for her formal education. However, she continued to pursue her academic interests within the confines of her home. If Mount Holyoke could not contain her free spirit and imagination, at home where she was her father's favorite daughter, she put up a sustained resistance for intellectual autonomy against her father who like all Victorian fathers felt that ambition in a daughter was both, debilitating and unseemly. (Martin 87) Her distaste for general housekeeping was compounded by her mother's unconditional commitment to her social and domestic obligations. Two things that Dickinson needed most were, filial approval and support for the full realization of her latent creative talent and more importantly, personal autonomy. However, she got neither. "My mother does not care for thought and father is too busy with his Briefs," she wrote to Higginson in 1862. (*L* 173) Even as late as 1870 she lamented that she "never had a mother. I suppose a mother is one to whom you hurry when you are troubled." (*L* 210) So overbearing were the impositions that her mother's indisposition had created for her that she unconsciously began to blame her mother: "like a perverse Cinderella . . . for the dust-and-cinders position to which she [had] been confined." (Bennett 23) Contrary to the fairy tale ending, marriage she knew would only confirm her in her hated fate. Although Dickinson knew the power of heterosexual love, its most debilitating social and psychological perils, especially loss of will and subordination to the dominant male terrified her. In "an eloquent and devastating evaluation," as Joanne A. Dobson terms it (Juhasz 81), she measured the possible psychical demands and price of marriage, in a tellingly intimate letter to her friend and confidant Susan Gilbert:

> How dull our lives must seem to the bride, and the maiden, whose days are fed with gold, and who gathers pearls every evening; but to the wife Suzie, sometimes the *wife forgotten*, our lives perhaps seem dearer than all others in the world; you have seen flowers at morning *satisfied* with the dew, and those same sweet flowers at noon with their heads bowed in anguish before the mighty sun; think you these thirsty blossoms will now need naught but—dew? No, they will cry for sunlight and pine for the burning noon, though it scorches them, scathes them; they have got through with peace—they know that the man of noon, is *mightier* than the morning and their life is henceforth to him. Oh, Suzie, it is dangerous, and it is all too dear, and the spirits mightier which we cannot resist. It does so rend me, Suzie, the thought of it when it comes, that I tremble lest at sometime I, too, am yielded up. (*L* 89)

Despite an awareness of the sexual pleasure of heterosexuality, implicit in the gathering of 'pearls' and the satisfaction of 'dew,' one may note that the dominant concern in the letter is with the subsumption of identity by these "thrusting spirits" and this she found threatening and "dangerous." This overwhelming concern for personal autonomy was quite emphatically voiced in poem after poem:

I'm "wife"—I've finished that—
That other state—
I'm Czar—I'm "Woman" now—
It's safer so—
How odd the Girl's life looks
Behind this soft Eclipse—
I think that Earth feels so
To folks in Heaven—now—
This being comfort—then
That other kind—was pain—
But why compare?
I'm "Wife"! Stop there! (*CP* 94)

Edward Dickinson's emotional inaccessibility too was obvious, for though he "was not severe" as Higginson remarked, he was "remote. He did not wish [his daughters] to read anything but the Bible." (*L* 210) That Edward Dickinson was ambivalent about his daughter Emily as a thinking woman, becomes clearly evident from her letter to Higginson wherein she confessed, "Father . . . buys me many Books—but begs me not to read them—because he fears they joggle the Mind." (*L* 173) Contrary to her portrait as painfully wounded and obsessed with deprivation, Dickinson was a woman whose personal dimensions could be very keenly felt in her household. Self-willed and very much in possession of herself, she was not to be easily subdued by an authoritative patriarch who was accustomed to issuing instructions and meeting with unquestioned compliance. Edward Dickinson gradually began to make several concessions; the most significant of which was allowing Emily to keep her own hours of writing. This hard-won recognition of her need to keep her own hours—unlike Ann Bradstreet who had to sacrifice sleep to write poetry—marked a major victory in her skirmishes for territory and autonomy. While her sister Lavinia dedicated herself to the everyday domestic labors which would free Dickinson to write, Dickinson herself who even in her middle years was not self-sacrificing, was mistress of the household breads and puddings and a skilled horticulturist who delighted in growing exotica in her New England home. When she was not writing, she was engaged in other decorative activities, which might have derived from her generative impulse and vision and as Martha Bianchi recollects in her memoir about her: "Aunt Emily stood for indulgence." (6) The focus in her life was on pleasure and not suffering. She had the best bedroom in the house—a sunny and spacious room overlooking the main street of Amherst. To this retreat she often retired to read Elizabeth Barrett Browning's *Aurora Leigh*, in which she found the model she had so long sought. Among others, she read the works of Shakespeare whom she admired immensely. "While Shakespeare remains Literature is firm," (*L* 214) she wrote. Her other reading included her contemporaries George Eliot, Carlyle, Emerson, Charlotte and Emily Bronte. Dickinson would often shut herself out in her room to pen heavily emended lyric poems about the experiences that most touched her life and the lives of her friends. Instead of socks and silks, she would darn these poems into booklets, which were only to be discovered after her death. While the "Gentlewomen" in "Plush" engaged themselves with corseting their bodies and "doing good" for their community, Dickinson watched ceaselessly from the relative *freedom* of her room, the life of *sober* Amherst go by. Her distaste for nineteenth century gender role expectations, among them the social activities that girls of her age engaged themselves in, comes across quite clearly when she writes:

> What Soft—Cherubic Creatures—
> These Gentlewomen are—
> One would as soon assault a Plush—
> Or violate a Star. (*CP* 191)

The years following her return to Amherst were years of expansion for Dickinson. Her health, which had suffered a setback at Mount Holyoke, improved and new books and interests absorbed her. The transatlantic influences, however, were not the only ones that marked her psychic geography. Her inner landscape was shaped as much by local conditions, as it was by her American inheritance. The example of Ann Bradstreet, who had led a demanding existence as the mother of eight children and the wife of a Puritan governor, would perhaps lend a clearer insight into these influences. In spite of burdensome domestic responsibilities and a relatively primitive environment, Bradstreet had managed to publish the first volume of poetry written by a woman in the New World in the seventeenth century. She had sometimes doubted the validity of the divine mission of the Puritans and even the existence of God, yet had ultimately learnt to control her agonizing skepticism by committing herself to the religious values of her culture. Dickinson, however, was much less committed to the morals of nineteenth century congregational Amherst and chose to listen to her inner voice instead. However, even though her privatism was in sharp contrast to Bradstreet's piety, both women were critical of the Puritan doctrine of manifest destiny. Among the girls she saw at this time, were Susan Gilbert and Emily Fowler with whom she shared confidences about her private aspirations. To Fowler she wrote in 1850 that her return to Amherst was marked by a time when "me and my spirit were fighting." (*L* 35) Dickinson was at that time, quite conscious that she "was highly accomplished and gifted" (*L* 22) and different from the other women around her. This admission, however, was not to be confused with arrogance but to be seen as her recognition of a latent talent that could possibly carve out for her, a future beyond the narrow confines of domesticity alone. It is quite evident from her letter to Abiah Root, that even while going through her routine domestic chores, the fertile mind of this "reclusive poet-cook" as Sandra Gilbert calls her (Juhasz 22), raced on furiously weaving golden dreams. Delighting most in whipping, punching, and kneading creams and doughs possibly for the vicarious satisfaction that the activity afforded, Dickinson rejected conventional piety and turned into "this wilderness life of mine" (*L* 40), instead of turning to Jesus of Nazareth for redemption:

> I am one of the lingering *bad* ones and so do *I* slink, praise and ponder, and ponder, and praise and do work with knowing why—not surely for *this* brief world, and more sure it is not for Heaven—and I ask what this message *means* that they ask for so very eagerly, *you* know of this depth, and fullness, will you *try* to tell me about it? (*L* 39)

Dickinson knew that she was exceptional and had the potential for being a great poet. The spiritual fervor generated by her unrealized capacities and the desire for recognition of her poet/self, both conscious and unconscious, must have been considerable. "Could I make you and Austin—proud—sometimes—a great way off—'twould give me taller feet," she wrote to Susan in the summer of 1861 (*L* 163), reiterating in a later poem:

> Fame of Myself, to justify,
> All other Plaudit be
> Superfluous—An Incense
> Beyond Necessity—
> Fame of Myself to lack—Although
> My Name be else Supreme—
> This were an Honor honorless—
> A futile Diadem. (*CP* 350-51)

Poetry she was convinced, could be the only vehicle for her self-realization and self-justification. However, as Dobson suggests, the "Promptings of the unconscious, the command of language, the relentless creation of the self in a medium that is alien to a pragmatic society, all these demand isolation and radical integrity, selfishness and courage . . . traits [that] have long been masculine *prerogatives* and Emily Dickinson was a lady." (Juhasz 89)

Nevertheless, Dickinson knew what she wanted and consciously chose a sequestered life. This was neither to be seen neither as a hermetic retreat nor as a spinsterish oddity. Her self-imposed seclusion included not only reading and correspondence but also a wide range of people whom she found intellectually stimulating and emotionally rewarding. As Wendy Martin rightly suggests: "hers was a private rebellion in the service of her poetry, not an exercise in self-effacement." (80) Her friends included men and women but her company as well as the dispensation of her time were judiciously monitored. Not given to traveling or receiving routine visitors, she was neither eccentric or quaint as some critics would have us believe; only determined to survive and to use her powers and inner resources constructively and efficiently. For the last twenty-five years of her life, Dickinson was socially reclusive and had withdrawn from village society after the Reverend Charles Wadsworth's removal to San Francisco in the spring of 1861 and Susan Gilbert's marriage to Austin. Yet, renunciation of the larger world had ensured her safety and stability in a world that was in constant flux. Her home, then, became her personal fixed center:

> By creating and safeguarding her privacy she made extraordinary discoveries unusual for any one in the nineteenth century. Not only did she pierce the mystifications of evangelical Christianity, as well as the mystique of redemptive femininity, but she also achieved a resolution of the mind/body dualism that prefigures twentieth century scientific findings. Most important, she evolved a complicated understanding of emotional dynamics that is startlingly modern. (Martin 81)

She was neither "partially cracked," as Higginson refers to her, nor "the climax of all the family oddity" as Mabel Loomis Todd, a family friend and Austin's mistress, wrote in 1881. Todd's reference to Dickinson as "the *character* of Amherst. . . . Whom the people call the *Myth*" and who "nobody ever sees" (quoted from Juhasz 43), did contribute in large measures towards "the process of mystification and fictionalization of the poet." However, Susan Gilbert sees in her seclusion "a process of self-mythologising that led Dickinson herself to use all the materials of her daily reality, and most especially the details of domesticity, as if they were not facts but metaphors, in order to recreate herself—and-her-life as a single emblematic text . . . structured . . . around a series of "mysteries" that were distinctively female, deliberately exploring and exploiting characteristics, even the constraints, of nineteenth century womanhood so as to transform and transcend them." (Juhasz 22)

On close perusal of her life and work, Emily Dickinson comes across as a strong, practical woman, exercising her gifts as she had to, making choices and seeking viable ways of self-empowerment. Against the expected passivity of a New England inheritance: "that mutilated its gifted women," (Juhasz 89) Dickinson pitted her alterity by withdrawing socially and by adopting strategies, in her life and art that would subvert and appropriate the dominant culture. She converted all the experiences and encounters of her life into metaphors and employed this metaphoric dialect to: "Tell all the Truth—but tell it slant":

Tell all the Truth—but tell it slant—
Success in Circuit lies
Too bright for our infirm Delight
The Truth's superb surprise
As Lightening to the Children eased
With explanation kind
The Truth must dazzle gradually
Or every man be blind. (*CP* 506-7)

Dickinson attempted to explore cultural and gender role expectations that induce female inhibitions, through a bipolar consciousness with which, she monitored at once her own exuberant imagination and the claustrophobic demands of her social and religious reality, as well as the judgment passed on her:

They shut me up in Prose—
As when a little girl
They put me in the Closet—
Because they liked me "still"—

Still! Could themselves have peeped—
And seen my Brain—go round—
They might as wise have lodged a Bird
For Treason—in the Pound—

Himself has but to will

> And easy as a Star
> Abolish his Captivity—
> And Laugh—No more have I. (*CP* 302)

The poem immediately sets up a polarity between "me" and "they" and the weight of the entire poem seems to rest on the word "still," which carries ironic implications of hope and despair, freedom and captivity, death and renewal. Scoffing at a wisdom that hopes to hold the "Brain" captive, the poem, reinforces the idea that freedom and captivity are an attitude, a state of mind and an act of will. "Life—is what we make it" (*CP* 343) and "Captivity is Consciousness/And so is Liberty" she wrote (*CP* 302). By adopting such poetic strategies, Dickinson attempted to dispense with time-honored authority in order to invent a brave new world inhabited by real women, doing and saying real things with a sense of authentic existence. Her vision was the creation of a world where women would be called upon to fulfill themselves as women, by realizing their own worth. In this impulse toward autonomy, her privacy became the power station from which she hoped to generate enough energy to illuminate lives:

> If I can stop one Heart from breaking
> I shall not live in pain. (*CP* 433)

Many and varied are the opinions that scholars and critics, both men and women have expressed about the possible wellsprings of Emily Dickinson's creativity, which lend further complexity and mystery to an already unfathomable poet. One can at best approach her tentatively, for it would be near impossible to relate the whole story, which seduces without offering complete satisfaction. Her psychoanalytical biographer, John Cody, traces her creativity to the "violent disharmonies and unceasing restlessness of her inner life." (Qtd. Juhasz 2) Cody also believes that Dickinson's inability to assume a normal female identity in the absence of a suitable role model in her mother, may have resulted in her trying to emulate a masculine role model. He contends that gender confusion led to a psychotic breakdown and subsequent creativity as a form of atonement for family tragedy and sexual response. What Cody is suggesting, then, is that Dickinson's poems were the outpourings of either an abnormal woman, or of one who was not reconciled to her sex. However, as Susan Juhasz significantly argues: "Freud's system articulates and enshrines the profoundly sexist norms of our patriarchal culture." (4) Also, Cody's description of Dickinson after the highly productive years of the 1860s as "loveless, excluded, almost burnt out as a poet, and reduced to the status of a queer, hypochondriac and depressed old maid," seems quite aptly astonishing to her (4). Contrary to Cody's argument, Dickinson's poetry gives evidence not only of a brilliant mind, but also of her celebration of womanhood and its elevating powers, through a recognition and understanding of her own interior strengths. Her gender, then, is not to be seen as a deterrent but as a positive stimulus to her art. That she exteriorized that power in masculine form is very natural, since the most powerful figures in a patriarchal culture have been men and her poetic powers would not have fitted in with the conventional ideology of womanliness. One had to speak masculinely in a phallocentric world. This could have also been what Juliet Mitchell refers to as the "hysteric's voice which is the *woman's masculine language* . . . talking about feminine experience. It's both simultaneously the woman [poet's] refusal of the woman's world . . . and her construction from within a masculine world of that woman's world. . . . It touches, therefore on the importance of bisexuality." (Lodge 427) This idea finds reinforcement in Wendy Martin's contention that Dickinson possibly referred to her creative impulse as male, like her British counterparts who consciously assumed male or at least neuter pseudonyms. Mary Ann Evans became George Eliot and Charlotte and Emily Bronte chose Currer and Elis Bell. Martin speculates with Adrienne Rich and Joanne Feit Diehl that Dickinson's "Master" letters might possibly "have referred to her own active creative self—her own inner agency which she feared would desert or destroy her." (103) Their belief runs contrary to Ruth Miller, David Higgins and Richard Sewall's suggestion that the recipient of Dickinson's "Master" letters was her friend and confidant Samuel Bowles, to whom the now forty-three year old poet had turned for "paternal guidance" after her father's death (Martin 100). As Dickinson wrote:

The Outer—from the Inner
Derives its Magnitude—
Duke or Dwarf, accordingly
As is the Central Mood—
The Inner—paints the Outer—
The Brush without the Hand—
Its picture publishes—precise—
As in the inner Brand. (*CP* 216)

Again, no specious old spinster bordering on the abnormal could have known and written about her volcanic impulses, her "big-bang theory of self-creation" (Wilt 153) in such controlled, understated yet emphatic terms:

The reticent volcano keeps
His never slumbering plan—
Confided are his projects pink
To no precarious man.
If nature will not tell the tale

Jehovah told her
Can human nature not survive
Without a listener?

Admonished by her buckled lips
Let every babbler be
The only secret people keep
Is Immortality. (*CP* 708)

About madness Dickinson wrote:

Much madness is Divinest Sense—
To a discerning Eye—
Much Sense—the Starkest Madness—

'Tis the Majority
In this, as All, prevail—
Assent—and you are sane—
Demur—you're straightaway dangerous—
And handled with a chain. (*CP* 209)

Dickinson was, therefore, neither an anachronism wandering between two worlds, nor was she powerless to be reborn. In fact a counter legend claims her to be a spirited, fiery-tempered poet-heroine who insisted on solitude as her only access to the raptures of art. She meant to keep herself mad. Having grown up doubting traditional Christian pieties and Miss Lyons' evangelical fervor, she sought divinity in herself, as well as in the radiance of the ordinary world of finite reality around her.

Dickinson's other biographer George Whicher too, adopts masculinist interpretations of her poetic impulse and traces the source of her creativity to the failure of her love affair with the married Revered Charles Wadsworth, among other influences. What is particularly interesting is that both biographers trace her creativity to external sources rather than to an inherent talent and treat her poetry as a form of redress. Most importantly, not only do both separate the woman from the poet and associate the writing of poetry with the masculine, they also consider the lyric an inappropriate medium for the fulfillment of a woman's true identity as a woman, for woman-poet was considered a contradiction in terms. Cody and Whicher both had, thus, failed to acknowledge that Dickinson was trying, in fact, to assume her own emotional and intellectual autonomy through her art:

> her own knowledge of, and responsibility for, what she did; trying to understand and interpret her acts according to her own terms . . . [and] recognize the power that she derived from creating a world in which she could be herself, from creating a self with which she could accomplish her best. (Juhasz 2)

Her poems then, are neither to be heard as the ejaculations of a hapless victim, nor to be interpreted as the maudlin outpourings of a jilted, gender-confused hypochondriac.

For Dickinson, the issue of womanhood was seldom one of equality with men and more a matter of woman's inherent worth. She equated liberation with self-sufficiency, self-definition and self-empowerment and no poem articulates her attempts to characterize the Vesuvian nature of the art she believed was hers, than 'My Life had stood—a Loaded Gun,' composed in 1863 when she was at the height of her poetic powers. I quote here, the poem in full:

My Life had stood—a Loaded Gun—
In Corners—till a Day
The Owner passed—identified—
And carried Me away—

And now We roam in Sovereign woods—
And now We hunt the Doe—
And every time I speak for Him—
And Mountains straight reply—

And do I smile, such a cordial light
Upon the Valley glow—
It is as a Vesuvian face
Had let its pleasure through—

And when at Night—Our good Day done—
I guard My Master's Head—
'Tis better than the Eider—Duck's
Deep Pillow—to have shared—

To foe of His—I'm deadly foe—
None stir the second time—
On whom I lay a Yellow Eye—
Or an emphatic Thumb—

Though I than He—may longer live
He longer must—than I—
For I have but the power to kill,
Without—the power to die. (*CP* 369-70)

The poem articulates Dickinson's pride, anger, self-centeredness, daring, sexual candor, emotional and intellectual assertions—responses conventionally associated with unfeminine thoughts, nevertheless, the only empowering ones. The "Soft-Cherubic Creature," the angel in the poem is dead. In its place is a woman who is redefining herself as a woman through a release of powerful energies. What Dickinson is doing in this poem is subverting the power of patriarchy by defining first, the source of that power lucidly and then appropriating that power by conforming to it. The poem is structured in a double and simultaneous movement, containing the voice of a writer who first writes about the dominant culture and then appropriates its empowerment traits. This strategy performs the dual function of affecting an awareness of the destructive nature of patriarchal power as well as the matriarch's ability to appropriate it for reconstruction. As Paula Bennett suggests: "embracing the true or unacceptable self appears to be the poem's *reason d'être* just as it is the *reason d'être* of Plath's last poem." (6) Her life is her weapon and her poems the ammunition with which she wages her battle for freedom. Her life itself was a strategy, a question of making choices and choices she did make. She chose her seclusion making a virtue out of Victorian necessity that laid restrictions on female activity. She chose her friends, she chose not to marry, she chose her company and most importantly, she chose her vocation as poet. Albeit she hid away the vast corpus of her poems to be discovered by posterity, yet even in this she had silently exercised her right to, both, silence and voice:

One Blessing had I than the rest
So large to my yes
That I stopped gauging satisfied
For this enchanted size—

It was the limit of my Dream—
The focus of my Prayer—
A perfect—paralyzing Bliss—
Contented as Despair—

I knew no more of Want—or Cold—
Phantasms both become

For this new Value in the Soul—
Supremest Earthly Sum. . . .
Why Floods be served to us—in Bowls—
I speculate no more. (*CP* 370-71)

It is always what is under pressure in us, especially under pressure of concealment that explodes in poetry. It is in this context that Karl Keller draws attention to the influence of New England Puritan theology on the development of Dickinson's poetic muse. In this particular configuration of gender, patriarchy and religion, the double-voiced discourse that feminist critics have associated with women's writing generally, works to vitiate assertions of the dominant culture. While it declares overt, strident warfare on the one hand, it adopts subversive understated, indirect, ironic tactics, on the other. Likewise, in Dickinson's poetry, while the feminist voice directed against patriarchy dominates a critique of New England Puritan laws is tucked away into the margins. This poem could serve as an appropriate illustration for her poetic strategies:

My Worthiness is all my Doubt—
His Merit—all my fear—
Contrasting which, my quality
Do lowlier—appear—

Lest I should insufficient prove
For His beloved Need—
The Chiefest Apprehension
Upon my thronging Mind—

'Tis true that Deity, to stoop
Inherently incline—
For nothing higher than Itself
Itself can rest upon—

So I—the undivine abode
Of His Elect Content—
Conform my soul—as 'twere a Church,
Unto Her Sacrament. (*CP* 368)

Through an engagement with the whole process of abrogation and appropriation, which forms part of a continuing struggle, Dickinson manifests not only the dynamics of patriarchal and Puritan domination, but also wages guerrilla warfare against that domination through the subversive maneuver of dissembling, mimicry, parody and self-effacing diminution. The silence of conformity becomes the voice that draws attention to the colonial bias of oppression even while it underscores the principle of difference, which lies at the heart of this construction as other. The poet draws up an ironic and complex contrast, between a stooping "Deity" that can rest upon nothing "higher than itself" and the "undivine abode," the woman with her upward gaze, between "His" unquestioned "Merit" and her doubtful "Worthiness" and between "His Elect Content" and her "Chiefest Apprehensions." Thus, Dickinson not only interrogates patriarchal assumptions and Puritan laws, but also investigates the axioms by which these codes are imposed and maintained. In her poetry the deconstructive and the political go hand in hand, to raise and transform consciousness.

The critic Karl Keller argues that under the Puritan dispensation emphasized in the early decades of the seventeenth century, woman was granted a creative stimulus in the pure meditative sense, within herself. As such, he traces Dickinson's Creative stimulus to her Puritan inheritance. A woman's power lay in conforming to her "soul" (13) and like Ann Bradstreet before her, Dickinson too was exalted as a woman by her Puritan faith, he suggests. The Puritan emphasis on self-sufficiency and responsibility was the mainspring of the dignity and liberation of women. Albeit both Dickinson and Bradstreet before her were eccentric, devious and rebellious against their condition and station, they had realized themselves as women through self-sufficient responsibility to their souls. "We dignify our Faith, when we cross the ocean with it," Dickinson had written to Susan once. (*L* 152) Keller explains convincingly that it is no "paradox that in the discipline of her Puritan inclination I found one of the sources of herself as a poet. Woman's 'emancipation' under early Puritanism lay in *her responsibility for herself.*" (my italics) The fundamental emphasis on individual salvation and its accompanying loneliness, self-sufficiency, self-reliance and risks—elevated her. Though the logic might escape us today, her piety was her freedom." (12)

The universal imperative of concern for one's own soul and the emphasis on fulfillment through faith, was the Christian orthodoxy that Dickinson abstracted. This enabled her "to affirm her personal existence not as a woman but as a being: the solitary woman with an aggressive creativity whose self-fulfillment as a woman was the earthly form she could make the grace of God take," says Keller (13).

It was Dickinson's conviction that her *faith* gave life to her as a person. She did not deny the hostility of her times but learnt to recognize it and *believed*, in spite of it. In spite of the violence to herself, her faith became a desperate battle for intellectual and emotional autonomy through the non-violent means of her art. And, for her the way to freedom was not through passivity and subservience. Despite cultural assumptions that emphasized male authority (Edward Dickinson was always issuing instruction even when away from home) and female compliance and associated "cerebral activity" with "impairment of the reproductive function" (Martin 88). Dickinson succeeded in warding off the damaging effects of a culturally imposed femininity by asserting her need for independence. Unlike Emily Norcross Dickinson who had succumbed to the *superior* will of Edward Dickinson after initial resistance, only to be afflicted with "acute neuralgia," Emily Dickinson remained firmly in control at home in defiance of cultural convention. A large number of Victorian women who had been reduced to insignificant and insubstantial positions in the household and whose experiences and preferences had been trivialized, had ironically enough been laid up with the malady that Dickinson's mother had been struck with. Its damaging effects, therefore, were clearly visible to her and she was determined not to be martyred at the altar of patriarchy. Consequently, she waged a silent, lonely and painful battle against passivity and weakness through concerted non-violent action that was to become an article of faith with her. In a short, tightly constructed poem on faith she claims:

To lose one's faith—surpass
The loss of an Estate
Because Estates can be
Replenished—faith cannot—
Inherited with life—
Belief—but once—can be—
Annihilate a single clause—
And Being's—Beggary. (*CP* 180)

Through skillful maneuvering and subversion of Christian contingency, Dickinson expressed faith in her own conviction and in her antinomian impulse, which alone could give her a sense of *worth*. Knowing that she had no chance of competing in a man's world except by complacent patriarchal condescension, she fell back on the world of her own inner resources, wherein lay her hope of survival on an artistic and spiritual plane. "Exhilaration-is-within," she wrote:

There can be no Outer Wine
So royally intoxicate
As that diviner Brand

The Soul achieves—Herself—
To drink—or Set away
For visitor—Or Sacrament—
'Tis not of Holiday

To stimulate a Man
Who hath the Ample Rhine
Within his Closet—Best you can
Exhale in offering. (*CP* 182-83)

Although like Bradstreet and others before her, Dickinson too could fit into the "Myth of Puritan Woman Raised to Creativity through Duty" and the "pressures of responsibility," (Keller 21) her creative stimulus is not to be traced only to this undercurrent in her culture. The complex connection between being a woman, a Puritan and a poet was not just an unconscious phenomenon but a conscious struggle to realize the Puritan promise of spiritual autonomy to women. She "Herself" then, became the essential she chose not to set away either for "Visitor," or "Sacrament," or "To stimulate a Man." This perhaps would explain in part, the private nature of her life and art. Of the seventeen hundred and seventy five poems she wrote, only five were published during her lifetime in the *Spring Field Republican* (ed. Samuel Bowles), *The Round Table* and *A Masque of Poets* and none with her consent. When the renowned literary critic T.W. Higginson had suggested that she delay the publication of her poems, she had sent him a quiet and composed reply. "I smile" she wrote, "when you suggest that I delay 'to publish'—that being foreign to my thought, as Firmament to Fin—If fame belonged to me, I could not escape her—if she did not, the longest day would pass me on the chase." (*L* 174) For the most part, she wrote in secret and guarded her poems even from her family although, apart from Higginson, she did occasionally show her poems to a close circle of friends that included Bowles, Dr. J.G. Holland and Helen Hunt Jackson. However, she did not believe in exposing or publishing private feeling. "How can you print a piece of your soul," she said (qtd. Martin 248). Perhaps she knew that her uttering would either not be understood at all, or misunderstood as the doleful outpourings of a lonely spinster pining away for an imaginary lover, or disillusioned with a life that had little to offer besides loneliness and heart-break.

Dickinson's belief in herself and her poetic powers went much beyond devotional duties, to an intense exploration of the "mysteries of human nature [which] surpass the 'mysteries of redemption' for the infinite we only suppose, while we see the finite." (*L* 217) After Bowles' departure for Europe in 1862, Dickinson had initiated a literary correspondence with Higginson, who quoted a similar idea in a letter to his wife, after his first visit to the poet. Recording her profound, visceral response to life, Higginson quoted her as saying: "I find ecstasy in living—the mere sense of living is joy enough." Again: "if I read a book [and] it makes my whole body so cold no fire ever can warm me I know *that* is poetry. If I feel physically as if the top of my head were taken off, I know *that* is poetry. . . . Truth is such a rare thing it is delightful to tell it." (*L* 208-9)

To tell the truth of her life and experiences is indeed what Dickinson strove for, even though it threatened to brand her as fey and abnormal. Tell the truth she would but indirectly, for any direct rendition would only confirm undiscerning impressions about her being the mad woman in the attic. She was far too enigmatic for any direct cross-examination. "My Business is Circumference," she had written to Higginson in July 1862 (*L* 178) articulating her passion for abstraction and expansion. Through years of experience and observation she was able to make connections between emotional states and attitudes of mind, map points of consciousness and determine the periphery of experience. This, perhaps, is what she meant by "circumference," which has taken decades to be recognized and understood. A still-growing tradition of scholarly and critical writings asserts not only her intellectual and artistic sophistication but also the validity of her seclusion as an imperative to artistic creation. Given her Romantic inheritance, Emily Dickinson's psychic geography is not to be traced to some romantic idyll, some midsummer night's dream, but in her painful and agonized struggle toward the realization of her full potential as a woman:

To put this world down, like a Bundle—
And walk steady, away,
Requires Energy—possible Agony—
'Tis the Scarlet Way

Trodden with straight renunciation
By the Son of God
Later, his faint Confederates

Justify the Road—

Flavors of that old Crucifixion—
Filaments of Bloom, Pontius Pilate sowed—
Strong Clusters from Barabbas' Tomb—

Sacraments, Saints partook before us—
Patent, every drop,
With the Brand of the Gentile Drinkers
Who indorsed the Cup. (*CP* 257-58)

Despite the image of the poet as a Christ-like figure, the poem is not really as pious as it looks. While still a young girl at Mount Holyoke, Dickinson had learnt to doubt traditional Christian pieties. Having refused to submit to Miss Lyon's evangelical fervor, like Wallace Stevens' Christian woman in "Sunday Morning," she sought divinity in her self and in the sacramental radiance of her finite reality. Like Wallace Stevens, she became the high priestess of mother earth, committing her life and art to the celebration of nature's power. In this context the poem becomes at once, a site of female meanings associated with pain, suffering, and betrayal on the one hand and, more significantly, of the myth of female divinity on the other. The poet represents herself as a woman addressing the mind of another woman, with no sense at all that her femininity constitutes any poetic disadvantage. The poem is a feminist recall of the "Flavors of that old Crucifixion," that ancient sacrifice of Christ which has lost relevance, for it explicitly argues that power, cruelty and betrayal are the prerogatives of men: "the Filaments of Bloom, Pontius Pilate sowed" and the "Gentile Drinkers . . . indorsed." Christ's innocence, powerlessness and deep sense of betrayal are paralleled with women like Hester Pryne who deliberately chose a strife-torn and provisional life, preferring to withdraw into the dark recesses of her own psyche to be resurrected into another state of being. In the poem, the myth of poet as divine visionary, has been transformed into a paradoxically powerful image of powerlessness, which immediately sets up a significant connection between power and pain, heroism and hurt, brilliance and agony.

Dickinson is also exploring in the poem, the romantic idea of transcendental intellectuality as exhilarating and enabling and arguing that women too can become transcendent subjects. Her declaration of the poet's transcendence is absolute in her belief that women too possessed and could participate in the faculty of imaginative perception, which was the romantic poet's prerequisite and perquisite.

Another significant aspect of Puritanism that was appropriated by Dickinson and other feminist writers after her, was grounded in the structural similarity of Puritan reformation and feminist transformation. The Puritan conviction that their struggle in the wilderness of the New World was a redemptive mission echoing the millennial ideal found a striking parallel in the feminist ideal of establishing a new social order. While the Puritans envisioned the regaining of a lost paradise in heaven, which was a womanless ideal, the feminists envisioned a paradise on earth established by the community of women who revered life and earth's fecundity and in which, nature and friendship were sacred. A process of consciousness-raising, through conflict and struggle, however, motivated both impulses. Unlike Bradstreet who chose heaven as an affirmation of life, Dickinson rejected patriarchal religion in favor of a personal morality and her temporal reality. Wendy Martin puts Dickinson's vision in correct perspective when she argues that Dickinson gave up the "illusion of a foreordained life [and] gained the power of her senses. . . . She used her autonomy to bend religious structures to meet her needs" (9). Rejecting all fathers—God, father, potential husband, literary preceptor, Dickinson devoted her life's energy to her poetry:

> I saw no Way—The Heavens were stitched—
> I felt the Columns close—
> The Earth reversed her Hemisphere—
> I touched he Universe—
>
> And back it slid—and I alone—
> A Speck upon a Ball—

Went out upon Circumference—
Beyond the Dip of Bell. (*CP* 180)

The "Circumference" she set out to explore, was the periphery of her own experience. Her withdrawal into privatism, which was initially prompted by the Victorian restriction on women's activities, was soon to develop into an empowering force. It enabled her not only to "pierce the mystification of evangelical Christianity as well as the mystique of redemptive femininity" (Martin 81) but also to evolve a complicated understanding of emotional dynamics, which helped in resolving her mind/body dualism. By carefully analyzing her emotions in all their conflicting, contradictory and extreme states in her hours of seclusion, Dickinson made a virtue of cultural necessity to create a cosmology in which "Consciousness replaces the soul, ecstasy parallels grace, human love replaces God's sanctification and friends form the community of saints; nature is paradise, home is heaven, language is sacramental, and experience crystallized in art creates the possibility of eternal life." (Martin 80) With a firm belief in the redemptive powers of poetry, Dickinson waged her lonely and painful battle against adolescent religious crisis, against an authoritative parent, against a conventional life of matrimony and against intellectual and emotional domination. In each stage significantly, the struggle was against a male adversary.

The most crucial and eventful year in Dickinson's life was 1862. In no other year did she write so much poetry and with so much conviction. The same year she wrote:

I'm ceded—I've stopped being Their's—
The name They dropped upon my face
With water in the country church
Is finished using now,
And they can put it with my Dolls, . . .

Baptised, before, without the choice,
But this time, consciously, of grace—
Unto supremest name—

Called to my Full—The Crescent dropped—
Existence's whole Arc, filled up,
With one small Diadem.

My second Rank—too small the first—
Crowned—Crowning on my Father's breast—
A half unconscious Queen—
But this time—Adequate—Erect,
With Will to choose, or to reject,
And I choose, just a Crown. (*CP* 247)

The poem heralds her unconditional commitment to poetry and her increasing sense of relational and literary autonomy. While her earlier baptism had been a passive ritual defining her culturally imposed identity, her second baptism is an entirely autonomous decision transmuting her from girl-child to a mature, self assured adult capable of a "Will to choose or reject." She awards herself the "Diadem" of a poet, with perfect control over her territory, which she has annexed from her detractors and will now govern from a position of "self-authored authority" to use Bennett's term (81). Her transmutation is now complete.

Dickinson's battle for emotional and intellectual autonomy climaxed in her final battle with her preceptor Higginson, over the value of her poetry. In another attempt to receive approval from a recognized authority after Bowles' departure to Europe in 1862, she wrote to Higginson, then rated among America's foremost critics and men of letters, on 15 April 1862. She had just read Higginson's advice in his "Letter to a Young Contributor," in the first issue of the *Atlantic Monthly* and was prompted to initiate a correspondence that was to last till her death in 1886. In her first letter marked by trepidation and doubt she has asked, "Are you too deeply occupied to say if my Verse is alive? . . . Should you think it breathed and had you the leisure to tell me, I should feel quick gratitude—If I make the mistake—that you dared to tell me—would give me sincere honor—toward you" (*L* 171). Pleading for an honest and true opinion and hoping that he would not betray her, she had enclosed four of her poems, which were promptly sent back to her after being subjected to "surgery" that she said, was not as painful as she had "supposed." (*L* 172) Despite Higginson's reference to her poems as "spasmodic" and "uncontrolled" she wrote back to him saying, "I have had few pleasures so deep as your opinion. . . . Would you have time to be the 'friend' you should think I need? . . . will you be my Preceptor, Mr. Higginson?" (*L* 174-75) "I had no Monarch in my life, and cannot rule myself, and when I try to organize—my little Force explodes—and leaves me bare and charred—I think you called me 'wayward.' Will you help me improve?" (*L* 178) Although Dickinson continued to seek Higginson's advice and write to him she was soon beginning to realize that she had to decide between his judgment and her own, about the value of her poetry. "I shall observe your precept—though I don't understand it always," she wrote in August. "I marked a line in One Verse—because I met it after I made it—and never consciously touch a paint, mixed by another person—I do not let go it, because it is mine." (*L* 178-79) This growing sense of security and self-confidence, is reflected in several letters and poems she wrote during the following years. In yet another letter to Higginson in July 1862, she wrote:

> Will you tell me my fault, frankly as to yourself, for I had rather wince than die. Men do not call the surgeon, to commend—the Bone, but to see it, Sir, and fracture within, is more critical. And for this, Preceptor, I shall bring you—Obedience— . . . and every gratitude I know. *Perhaps you smile at me. I could not stop for that*—My business is Circumference—An ignorance, not of Customs, but if caught with the Dawn—or the Sunset see me—Myself the only Kangaroo among the Beauty, Sir, if you please, it afflicts me, *and I thought that instruction would take it away.* (*L* 176, my italics)

The same confidence is reflected in her letter to the Hollands in which she writes, 'perhaps you laugh at me! Perhaps the whole United States are Laughing at me too! *I* can't stop for that! *My* business is to love. . . . "*My* Business is to *sing*."' (*L* 177) In sharp contrast to Higginson's opinion that Dickinson's poems were not fit for publication, Helen Hunt Jackson, the only woman poet that Dickinson knew besides Barrett Browning and the Brontes, appreciated her poetry and wanted the public to read it. Dickinson sought Higginson's advice on Jackson's offer to publish some of her poems: "in the shelter of double anonymity" but he failed either to give her useful advice or to encourage her to publish. Significantly, Dickinson's poem, 'Success is counted sweetest' which appeared in *The Masque of Poets* was one of the two poems that were singled out for praise by the reviewer of the *New York Times* (Leyda 302). What is worth mentioning here, is that fortunately or unfortunately, Dickinson had repeatedly placed herself at the mercy of powerful males whose judgment she was prepared to accept. After her first "tutor" Benjamin Franklin died, she had turned to Bowles. The five poems that Bowles had published in the *Springfield Republican* were not even the ones she had given him herself and had appeared in a modified form, to boot. Bowles had made substantive changes because he thought he knew better than she and perhaps because he could not trust her ingenuity and her abilities. However, when Bowles published 'The Snake' in the 17 February 1866 issue of the *Springfield Weekly Republican*, she was quick to complain to Higginson. In a letter appended with a clipping of the poem, she protested that in the process of the *improvemental* changes that either Bowles or Josiah Holland had made, the poem "was robbed of me—defeated too of the third line by the punctuation. The third and fourth were one." (*L* 192) The letter clearly indicated her disapproval of the *corrections* in imagery, rhythm and punctuation. Her version, which read:

A narrow Fellow in the grass
Occasionally rides—
You may have met Him—did you not
His notice sudden is—

was changed to:

You may have met him—did you not?
His notice instant is. (Qtd. Keller 199)

Bowles, Holland, Higginson, had all amply demonstrated how the dominant group exercises its literary hegemony and pushes its women geniuses into personal and literary isolation. Although Higginson admired: "the rare sparkles of light . . . that fine edge of thought . . . which . . . would be so easy . . . to miss" (*L* 198), and Bowles and Holland too, acknowledged Dickinson's intellectual capabilities, they could not accord her work unalloyed praise. It was, in fact, Dickinson's women acquaintances and friends—Sue Dickinson, Lavinia Dickinson, Helen Jackson, Mabel Loomis Todd, Martha Bianchi—who saved her and offered the approval and support she sought.

Among other nineteenth century women who had explored the issues of autonomy and relationship was Margaret Fuller. She had stated in *Woman in the Nineteenth Century* (1845), the first mature consideration of feminism by an American touching every aspect of the subject, intellectual, economic, political, sexual, that men in highly polarized societies had been conditioned to perceive woman as "the other." They could, neither understand and appreciate their need for self-development nor were reliable guides. She insisted that because "not one man, in the million, . . . not in the hundred million, can rise above the belief that women was made *for man*," woman would have to "lay aside all thought, such as she habitually cherished, of being taught and led by men." (qtd. Kolodny 355) Alternately, Fuller advised that women seek their counsel and tap their own inner resources to achieve "inward and outward freedom [which] for woman as for man shall be acknowledged as a right, not yielded as a concession." (26) Whether Dickinson had read Fuller's book or not is not certain, but disappointed at Higginson's failure to recognize and nurture her creative talent, she had probably understood intuitively, the full import of Fuller's contention and advice. She began to depend increasingly on her own judgment regarding both, the value of her poetry, as well as her desire despite being misunderstood or ignored, to reveal through the poems she continued to write, a responsive and wholly alive consciousness. In her attempts to brace and order her internal power against continued threats to her autonomy, Dickinson made language her strongest weapon. The Word became her chief defense against her adversaries:

> A Word that breathes distinctly
> Has not the power to die
> Cohesive as the Spirit
> It may expire if He—
> "Made Flesh and dwelt among us"
> Could Condescension be
> Like this consent of Language
> This beloved Philology. (*CP* 676)

By appropriating the Word of God and making it her own, by choosing the power of the human word over the divine, she invested the human word, "the Word made Flesh" with God-like authority. This transference of power, then, became her criterion for measuring all power outside the self. By drawing upon the authority of Christian orthodoxy, Dickinson created an alternate power "potentially subversive of any external authority based on the sovereignty of a male-identified divinity." (Juhasz 157) 'A Word Made Flesh' in Joanne Feit Diehl's opinion, can be viewed as "Dickinson's central statement about language, her role as poet, and her relationship to the Divine." (Juhasz 158) Language became her most potent weapon and shield against estrangement and alienation. The ground of poetry alone, then, could have offered Dickinson the freedom to articulate her independence. In her art she was master of herself, whatever that self was, however unwomanly, aggressive or even inhuman society may judge it to be.

Works Cited

Bennett, Paula. 1986. *My Life a Loaded Gun: Female Creativity and Feminist Poetics.* Boston: Beacon Press.

Bianchi, Martha. 1932. *Emily Dickinson Face to Face: Unpublished Letters with Notes and Reminiscences.* Boston and New York: Houghton Mifflin.

Cody, John.1971. *After Great Pain: The Inner Life of Emily Dickinson.* Cambridge, Massachusetts: Harvard Univ. Press.

Dickinson, Emily. *The Complete Poems of Emily Dickinson*, ed. Thomas H. Johnson. Boston: Little Brown Press. 1960. Hereafter cited as *CP.*

______. *Emily Dickinson: Selected Letters.* Ed. Thomas H. Johnson. Cambridge, Massachusetts: The Belknap Press of Harvard University. 1971.

Diehl, Joan Feit. "Ransom in a Voice: Language as Defense in Emily Dickinson's Poetry." *Feminist Critics Read Emily Dickinson.* 156-75.

Dobson Joanne A. "Oh, Suzie, it is Dangerous: Emily Dickinson and the Archetype." *Feminist Critics Read Emily Dickinson.* 80-95.

Gilbert, Sandra. "The Wayward Nun Beneath the Hill: Emily Dickinson and the Mysteries of Womanhood." *Feminist Critics Read Emily Dickinson.* 22-44.

Juhasz, Susan. Ed. 1983. *Feminist Critics Read Emily Dickinson.* Bloomington: Indiana Univ. Press.

Keller, Karl. 1979. *The Only Kangaroo among the Beauty: Emily Dickinson and America.* Baltimore and London: The John Hopkins Univ. Press.

______. "Notes on Sleeping with Emily Dickinson." *Feminist Critics Read Emily Dickinson.* 67-79.

Kolodny, Annette. "Feminist Literary Criticism." *Critical Inquiry.* Autumn 1975. 75-92.

______. "Inventing a Feminist Discourse: Rhetoric and Resistance in Margaret Fuller's *Woman in the Nineteenth Century.*" *New Literary History: A Journal of Theory and Interpretation.* Vol. 25, no. 2. Spring 1994. 355-82.

Leyda, Jay. 1960. *The Years and Hours of Emily Dickinson.* 2 Vols. New Haven: Yale Univ. Press.

Lodge, David. Ed.1988. *Modern Criticism and Theory: A Reader.* New York: Longman.

Martin, Wendy. 1984. *An American Triptych: Anne Bradstreet, Emily Dickinson and Adrienne Rich.* Chapel Hill and London: The Univ. of North Carolina Press.

Mitchelle, Juliet. "Femininity, Narrative and Psychoanalysis." *Modern Criticism and Theory.* 425-30.

Ossoli, Margaret Fuller. 1971. *Woman in the Nineteenth Century and Kindred Papers.* New York: W.W. Norton.

Rich, Adrienne. "Vesuvius at Home: The Power of Emily Dickinson." *On Lies Secrets and Silence: Selected Prose 1966-1978.* New York: W.W. Norton. 1979. 157-74.

Whicher, George. 1938. *This Was a Poet: A Critical Biography of Emily Dickinson.* Ann Arbor: Univ. of Michigan Press.

Wilt, Judith. "Emily Dickinson: Playing House." *Boundary* (Winter 1984), Vol.12, no.2, 153-69.

Songs of Vision, Valor and Faith: Sarojini Naidu

Into the strife of the throng and the tumult,
The war of sweet Love against folly and wrong;
Where brave hearts carry the sword of battle,
'Tis mine to carry the banner of song

Sarojini Naidu

Even while Emily Dickinson waged a silent but resolute and relentless war for personal and literary autonomy in the midst of a rigid and claustrophobic Puritan patriarchy, across continents and cultures and closer to home was another ardent crusader for women's rights in the figure of Sarojini Naidu. Hailed as the nightingale of India, Sarojini was unlike the reclusive Emily, an important public figure and an active participant in the struggle for women's emancipation in pre- and post-independent India. Although she often clarified that she was not a feminist because India did not need Western-style feminism, there are discernible in her poetry, distinct undercurrents of a desire to break free of conventionally accepted and expected norms of Indian womanhood. And what better evidence could there be than the unconventional life-style that she herself had adopted.

Descending from a long line of Sanskrit scholars who taught the scriptures, Sarojini was the eldest of the eight children of Dr. Aghorenath Chattopadhaya and Varda Sundari. While her father was a brilliant dreamer-scientist, writer of Urdu and Bengali poetry, pioneer of India's freedom struggle and crusader for women's education and widow re-marriage, her mother was a singer and poet in her own right. Born on Feb.13, 1879 at Hyderabad and brought up in the best traditions of her highly cultured and honored family, Sarojini was fed on a liberal education that was free from religious and caste prejudices. She thus imbibed the best of the Hindu and Muslim cultures, as well as the Western education she was exposed to and also acquired great linguistic skill in English and Bengali, alongside learning Urdu and Persian, the influence of which is quite evident in her poetry and other writings. Having achieved top honors in Madras Presidency in the Matriculation examination at the young age of twelve, she composed her first poem at the age of eleven. She says she was "sighing over a sum of Algebra [that] wouldn't come right," when she wrote out instead, "a whole poem" that came to her "suddenly." (Symons 17) Even as a child Sarojini was spirited enough not to submit to a regimen dictated by her father who wanted to decide what she would learn or not learn. Although her father, she stated,

> was determined that I should be a great mathematician or a scientist . . . the poetic instinct which I inherited from him and also from my mother (who wrote some lovely Bengali lyrics in her youth) proved stronger. (Symons 11)

However, the poem which formally inaugurated her poetic career was a long thirteen hundred-line poem a la 'Lady of the Lake,' which she wrote in six days at the age of thirteen. Published as *Mehir Muneer: A Poem in Three Cantos by a Brahmin Girl* in 1883, the poem is an adaptation of one of Sir Edwin Arnold's stories, as Izzat Yar Khan tells us (6). It ostensibly revolves around the enchanted world and love of Mehir Muneer and Badar Muneer "The Pure Ideal," "without peer," of Mehir Muneer's "dream." Very early in life then, Sarojini had consciously articulated through the poem, her poetic propensities and a latent desire for ideal love. On the sub-textual level, Mehir Muneer could very well have been identified with the poetic passion that she longed to be claimed by. She wished for

> No rich brocade no priceless gem,
> No radiant, brilliant diadem. (56)

but only her "sov'reign" great with whom she could sing her songs of divine love. Although the poem has a dream-like quality, it does reveal the poet's nascent underpinnings and secret desire to be recognized as a poet of merit. Again, in 'On My Birthday,' a poem composed on her fourteenth birthday she wrote:

> My joys were not what joys to childhood seem:
> Not on unthinking sports my soul fed—
> But nursed it was on many a brighter theme,
> And lofty high ideals formed my radiant dreams. (Qtd. Mishra 30)

Although the poem is unarguably Wordsworthian in tone, it illustrates that poetry for Sarojini was not just the articulation of her sensuous psyche. Mehir Muneer won her an annual scholarship of 300 pounds from the Nizam of Hyderabad, for pursuing higher studies in England. At a time when women were still struggling for their right to basic education, Sarojini had earned the privilege of attending lectures at King's College, University of London and Girton College, Cambridge University, although serious illness prevented her from earning any degree from either institution. However, while in England, she met Sir Edmund Gosse, Arthur Symons and other members of the Rhymers Club from whom she learnt the verbal felicity, metrical discipline and musical texture so evident in her poetry and continued to write poems throughout her stay abroad. The poems written during these years were later published privately by her father in a volume entitled *Songs* (1895). After traveling widely on the European continent, she returned to India in 1898, to marry Dr. M. Govindarajulu Naidu, a widower ten years her senior, in a controversial inter-caste marriage. She was a Brahmin, he was not. One of the possible reasons for her being sent off to England could have been this love affair, which had raised several eyebrows and objections, both within and outside the family. The move, however, had left Sarojini more determined than ever before in her resolve to marry the man she loved. In the years following her marriage, Sarojini slipped quietly into the expected role of wife and keeper of Dr. Naidu's household and mother to her four children who were born soon after in quick succession. However, her restless spirit could not be contained for long. She was soon persuaded by Gopal Krishna Gokhale, to step out of her household and participate more actively in the public life of the nation. Subsequently, during the course of these public appearances and political meetings, she came in close contact with several leading personalities of the freedom movement—Lokmanya Tilak, Jawaharlal Nehru, Mohammad Ali Jinnah, Uman Sobani a Bombay businessman, and most importantly, Mahatma Gandhi. These men greatly influenced her life and she gained immense strength from her association with them. Ironically enough, it was with the tacit approval and support of these men that she could challenge patriarchal assumptions and thus provide impetus to the women's movement.

Sarojini's first volume of poetry *The Golden Threshold*, which was to set the tone and mood of her subsequent volumes, was published in 1905 to be followed by *The Bird of Time* (1912), and *The Broken Wing: Songs of Love, Death and the Spring* (1915-1916). These volumes were later edited into a single volume, *The Sceptred Flute: Songs of India* (1928). Her unpublished poems were published posthumously as *The Feather of the Dawn* (1961), by her daughter Padmaja Naidu, twelve years after her death. When Sarojini the politician was invented, Sarojini the poet died, for poetic career was cut short at the young age of thirty-eight on being drawn into the vortex of the Indian National Movement. Yet, her prose writings and public speeches too, published as *Speeches and Writings of Sarojini Naidu*, could very well be defined as highly inspired poems in prose. Her biographer Tara Ali Baig writes that she "produced an extra-ordinary effect upon her audience wherever she spoke." (64) An important figure in the recent history of India, she is remembered as the first woman President of The Indian Congress, the first woman Governor of Uttar Pradesh and as India's cultural ambassador who avidly mobilized support for India's freedom abroad. However, she must also be remembered as a poet, activist and passionate advocate of women's rights and emancipation. As she wrote in a poem:

With frugal skill her simple wants she tends . . .
Ere the quick night upon her flock descends
Like a black panther from the caves of sleep. (70)

Closely related to this struggle was her association with and belief in the ideological principles of Gandhi whom she had first met in 1914 in London. Even though the former lived a life of austerity and Sarojini was a lively poet fond of the good things of life, the two struck an instant rapport. This was to fructify later into a life-long association through the pursuance of a mutual desire and goal. Both were messengers of peace and harmony and the poet had immense faith in Gandhi's leadership. She had eulogized Gandhi on his death in her elegiac speech, "My Father Do not Rest," declaring passionately: "Our sword is the sword of the spirit that conquers without blood." (193) When the little man was sent to prison in 1922 for spearheading the *Satyagraha* (non-violence) movement, his parting words to her: "I entrust the destiny of India in your hands" had echoed her own sentiment. (Qtd. *IAP* 174) Nevertheless, despite the significant role that the poet had played in the public life of pre- and post-independent India, it was in her poetry that she lived out and enacted an inner life from which flowed her outer life that had touched the life of the nation.

Since the value of Sarojini's poetry lies in its historical and ideological significance, its evaluation requires a historical rather than a literary perspective, as well as an insight into its underlying ideology of equality, freedom, peace and harmony. There has been renewed interest in her poetry in recent years, more so by women scholars, to emphasize how her art has been systematically devalued by modernist writers who have dismissed it as representing a dead aesthetic. However, there is more to her poetry than just her sensual flights of fancy into imaginary lands in the manner of Keats and Coleridge. Her poetic agenda is subtly discernible in the many ways in which she subverts and appropriates inherited literary and cultural traditions even while remaining within the cultural mainstream. Although her poetry has been variously defined as melodious and "unoriginal" (Sarang 2), romantic, recondite, excessively "exuberant" and lacking in "high reflective moments" (Dwivedi qtd. Mishra 66), and "intellectual fibre " (Naik 8), the historical and cultural relevance of her poetry seems to have escaped the attention of her detractors. P. Lal, Nissim Ezekiel, R. Parthasarthy, Adil Jussawala, Keki Daruwalla and other critics belonging to a whole new generation of modern poets have debunked her poetry as representing a decadent romanticism of a particularly meretricious kind. This is, Chavan believes, "because of their sense of commitment to reality about the self and the environment." (12) Jussawala thought Sarojini was a fine person but "wrote some atrocious verse. And it needed saying when [she] wrote it." (66) A.K. Mehrotra has even gone to the extent of anthologizing one of her poems "as an example of everything a poem should *not* be" (emphasis added 14). This is a harsh judgement indeed. Again, in her book *The Fair Voice: A Study of Indian Women Poets*, S.P. Chavan has stated that Sarojini's poetry becomes "a relevant activity for her only because it fulfills the need of her essentially sensuous and musical psyche," (27) for it "bypass[es] the tensions of [her] personal [life] and social milieu." (28) Nevertheless, it must be remembered that contrary to Chavan's argument, Sarojini was a social activist who had adopted the medium of poetry in pursuance of a social agenda. Having been associated with the women's cause not as just an activist but as a legislator also, it had become for her an emotional issue so that even her speeches had become poetic in tone. The charge of a "decadent" romanticism, "because of her infatuation for the music of words" (Chavan 28) also, seems quite unjustified for the poet's passion for words could be seen as an attempt to explore the liberating and empowering potential of language. This same love of words could have possibly been a poetic strategy too for highlighting by contrast, the centuries of silence that women had been pushed into.

One is tempted to suggest that Sarojini's reputation as a leading political figure, could possibly have been an image trap set up by the men who wished to tokenize her as a woman. A woman poet was never really taken seriously (as in her mother's case before her) and as such, she had no significant role to play. Poetry seemed more of an indulgence especially when there was more important work to be done. Likewise, her reputation as a poet rests largely on patriarchal and intellectually elitist notions of greatness. In this context, the influence of Gosse comes to mind as ready illustration. Sarojini had considered Gosse "the rarest and most gifted of [geniuses]" (Qtd. Paranjape 8) and had at his behest stopped being "a clever machine-made imitator of the English classics." (Gosse 5) His contention was, that although her poems were "skilful in form, correct in grammar and blameless in sentiment, . . . they had the disadvantage of being totally without individuality." (4) However, despite the influence of the dominant transcultural ideologies of her time and the men in her life and contrary to Gosse's opinion, there is a clearly identifiable stamp of Sarojini the woman on her poetry. Born a dreamer like her father and mother and fed on a staple of tolerance and communal harmony, she dared to envision a world governed by equality and justice. As she writes in *Nilambuja* a beautiful piece of prose, the woman protagonist in the "infinite loneliness of her soul's ecstasy for Beauty," stands "alone in the temple of her dreams, leaning out into the darkness . . . with the weariness of a futile, striving to pluck an unattainable desire" (*Nilambuja* 133). One of her most urgent dreams besides that of national freedom was to witness an era, as she declared in her speech 'Indian Women and the Franchise,' when women would be able to appeal to men's "sense of justice" and not their "chivalry" (158).

'Nilambuja: The Fantasy of a Poet's Mood' (133-35) is a poetic fantasy in the manner of 'Kubla Khan' and represents a series of potent visionary images suggesting utopian themes of eternity and change. Inside her temple of dreams which, like Coleridge's "pleasure dome," promises growth and color:

> the lyric child standing in the desert of her lonely temperament, watching the stars, [dares to catch] from their inaccessible fires the soaring flame of a manifold enthusiasm, a myriad-hearted passion for humanity, for knowledge, for life, above all, for eternal beauty of the Universe. Thenceforth she [moves] in the shadow of mystery, consumed with a deep intellectual hunger, an unquenchable spiritual thirst, forever seeking the ecstasy of Beauty in the voice of the winds . . . but most of all in the touching beauty of human faces and the secret poetry of every human life. (134)

'Nilambuja,' which means 'blue lotus,' could well be interpreted as a poetic self-portrait, a symbolic fulfillment of the poet's needs, a mythical being invented to give solace in an otherwise terrifying situation. Sarojini's poetry then, is to be seen not only as the articulation of her Byzantine dreams but also as a covert expression of the secret yearnings of her deepest desires. She regrets that she could not, however, find the right voice for "the music of her inner voices so importunate in their cry for expression." (*Nilambuja* 134) Her true thoughts and emotions were thus stifled by the 'norms' of good writing established by society, as well as a literary patriarchy that prescribed and proscribed, how and what to write. Her valued and trusted advisor Arthur Symons, too, had damned her with faint praise by ascribing her talent to a "rare temperament, the temperament of *a woman of the East*." (Symons 10, my italics) There was much more to this seemingly harmless comment than just marginalizing her to the status of a narrow, provincial writer. Symons had exposed her art, thereby, to the constant threat of propaganda and phony Indianness eminently entitled for export. Likewise, Gosse had also cleverly pushed her into an image trap by asking her not to write about "skylarks in a landscape of our Midland countries," but to showcase India. He asked her to "introduce us to the vivid populations of her own voluptuous and unfamiliar province; in other words, to be a genuine Indian poet of the Deccan." (Gosse 5) Unfortunately, this was a suggestion Sarojini had readily though somewhat unwittingly succumbed to. The trap, as Paranjape rightly suggests, "was to give to the West the picture of India which the West wished to see." (12) This conscious deference to male advice and opinion could be ascribed to both, an intense and direct exposure to the Western influence under which women's education was given impetus, as well as to the poet's essentialist construction of femininity and masculinity. However, despite endorsing patriarchy through her image of conventional and subordinate women, besides reflecting other concerns, her poems are a salutation to "the laughter and beauty of women long dead." (58) One agrees with Paranjape that there is something "undeniable and uniquely feminist in her aesthetics. Sarojini's deliberate espousal of ephemerality and her cultivated anti-intellectualism aligns her to all those women whose voices and words were lost, who were outside the purview of the high-brow, male-dominated notions of great art." (18)

This contention is lent further credence by some of the blatantly candid observations the poet had made in some of her speeches. While speaking at Allahabad on the postponement of all recruitment of Indian indentured labor, she had stated passionately: "Let the blood of your hearts blot out the shame your women have suffered . . . *I feel the dishonor offered to me in the dishonor to my sex*. Is national righteousness possible when the men of India sit still and see such crimes?" (Qtd. Mishra 37, my italics)

A society alters its definition of what is appropriate, just as it alters its definition of how artists may express themselves, albeit the commonly accepted rules of discourse may be different for men and women. These 'norms' are important determinants in defining the parameters of what can be expressed, revealed or even admitted as true or meaningful. And 'norms' are never neutral or universal but governed by the specific *requirements* of a class or society. What Sarojini had expressed was what she had been *expected* to or been able to express in her historical time and space. The complex interplay of innate biological determinants, personal propensities, talent, opportunities and the larger effects of socialization, were important determinants in laying down the limits of her expression and experience itself. However, even though the poet could never be dubbed as rebel or deviant, she could never become an ornamental symbol of patriarchal society. She strove to make choices in a milieu where few choices existed. Indian society has always been rooted in hierarchy. If within the family it has been age, sex, ordinal positions, affinal relationships, within the community it has been caste, lineage, learning, wealth, occupation, linkage with the ruling party and many such elements that have defined the rules of hierarchy. All these have been integrated by means of a complex combination of customs, functionality and religious norms unique to India and unknown anywhere else in the world. Consequently, even while she actualized herself, Sarojini carried on a woman's primary responsibilities of fulfilling her conjugal obligations including childbearing, rearing and holding the family together. And this in the cultural understanding of Indians was identified with femininity. She thus became a role model for other women by instilling in them a positive sense of feminine identity. This sense of identity, however, was not dependent on men or on the double standards of a male-dominated society. Ostensibly restricting herself to the roles assigned to her and without being aggressive, she redefined these roles by living on her own terms. Even while conforming to conventional and essentialist notions of femininity, she remained in perfect charge of her life and pursuits.

Sarojini's poetry thus chronicles much more than just a search for "the instincts of her awakening womanhood for the intoxication of love and the joy of life." It is a record of the "more urgent and intimate need of the poet-soul for perfect sympathy with its incommunicable vision, its subtle and inexpressible thoughts." (*Nilambuja* 135) Even though she had ceased to write poetry upon entering the political life of the nation, her speeches expressed the same longing for an ideal state in which, women and men of all classes, race and nationality could live by mutually extendable principles of justice. Putting her western experience to constructive use, she espoused the cause of women's education by working ceaselessly and relentlessly in that direction. She believed that "the crowning triumph of education," which was "the spiritual safeguard of the emancipated," would be "the complete emancipation of Indian womanhood." A liberal education was the only "wizard element that [could] reconcile and harmonize the natural conflict of races and religions." It would teach "the unity of a common source that underlies all divisions of race and the central truth that harmonizes all superficial differences of dogma." ('Women's Education and the Unity of India' 138)

Along with the struggle for equal educational opportunities for women, was Sarojini's untiring battle for women's franchise. Inspired as it was by the aggressive suffragette movement in England, the movement in India was nevertheless peaceful and non-violent. Allaying all culturally conditioned fears of women being divested of their "feminine graces" if they were given franchise, she reiterated:

> Indian woman is *essentially conservative* in her impulse and inspiration, and so far from demanding an alien standard of emancipation, she desires that her evolution should be no more than an ample and authentic efflorescence of an age long ideal of *dedicated service* whose roots are deep hidden in the past. ('Indian Women and the Franchise,' 162, my italics)

Sarojini's speeches thus served the dual function of allaying patriarchal apprehensions of women's rebellion against their hithherto unquestioned authority, even while they highlighted the circumscription of female activity to home, hearth and bedroom. She was in possession of a history as well as mythology, a learned as well as an oral tradition that supported ideas of inheritance, order, and possibilities for the true governance of India. Even while articulating and confirming male hegemonic positions, she silently reaffirmed, through careful manipulation and strategy, the unequal terms and ironic inconsistencies inherent in accepted customs. It was ironic, she argued, that women who were "Goddesses" and "high priestesses" within the "shelter of their homes," (161) were considered unfit to occupy positions in the "civic and spiritual life of the nation." (162) She thus evolved a mode that "mediated between the security of a comfortable patriarchy and the liberating power of the women's movement." Consequently, her texts too demonstrated "both resistance with and co-optation by the dominant ideology of her time which was colonialism." (Paranjape 7)

In the historical context, although Sarojini belonged among the first wave feminists who sought equal opportunities for women in education, franchise and employment, her feminism extends well beyond her historicity to encompass the larger concern of women's struggle for emancipation in every sphere of activity. Like most pre-Independence Indian poetry in English, even though her poetry is Romantic and Victorian in spirit and dominated by patriotic zeal and spiritual abstractions, there are a large number of poems and prose passages in her oeuvre that underscore a deep and abiding concern for social justice and reconstruction. In her writings, fiction goes hand in hand with history, now mirroring it now transforming it, so that the narrative of her poetry becomes a means of national identity and self-assertion. The ambiguous ways, in which she connects with the traditions she has inherited, can be seen best by examining some of her poems in detail.

The Golden Threshold opens with one of Sarojini's most widely acclaimed and anthologized poems, 'Palanquin-Bearers.' (58) The poem has been appreciated, for its artistic achievements in terms of intricate metrical composition and rhythmic consonance. It delightfully fuses "the palanquin, the bearers, the lady inside, the song and the springy movement," says Mishra. (75) Paranjape, on the other hand, criticizes the poem for leaving out the "sweat, toil and oppression of the palanquin bearers," which creates "a tension between the texture and structure of the poem." (212) In his book *The Renaissance of India*, James Cousins argues that the poem "rests on *no more substantial basis* than the likening of a lady to a flower, a bird, a star, a beam of light and a tear: *there is not a thought* in it." (259-60, my italics) He does, however, grudgingly grant it "instantaneous charm." While critics like Mishra, Cousins and Dwivedi, to name a few, have emphasized the *charm* of the lady and the poem, others like Paranjape have criticized the "pretty picture" that the poet presents of "a dying feudal order under colonialism." (212) Even while upholding the authenticity of setting, he highlights instead, the plight of the palanquin bearers. What is more significant however is, that both her detractors as well as supporters have tacitly, though unwittingly, acknowledged the corroding powers of patriarchy by recognizing the feudal basis of that power. Their criticism pre-supposes a life of luxury and pleasure for the silent occupant of the palanquin by smothering and swathing her identity in the veils of feminine charm and grace while her emotions and apprehensions largely remain unconsidered and unexplored. Although on the surface, the poet remains rooted in the mainstream and employs the traditionally romantic notion of an ostensibly starry-eyed, bejeweled and bedecked bride being borne on the shoulders of the beleaguered bearers to the home of an unknown lord and master, the poem silently articulates a hidden agenda. This is discernible in its very imagery, which shifts from flight to fall, freedom to confinement, animate to inanimate. The laughter is transformed into a tear, the swaying flower into a hanging star and the skimming bird into a 'puppet' "on a string." The "blooming beauty," to quote Dwivedi's epithet (67), could possibly be euphemistic of a child-bride, so that the palanquin itself seems to take on ominous and sepulchral dimensions. Even while showcasing a social custom associated with color and festivity, the palanquin becomes Sarojini's most powerful symbol of oppression and confinement. Tucked away into the margins of this text, then, is a critique of those social conventions, customs and norms of a patriarchal code that subdue and marginalise women through unquestioned compliance and confinement. The fate of the woman hangs precariously on the shoulders of men—father, brother, husband, son—from birth, through wedlock, unto death. In the Indian cultural understanding marriage was considered a new birth, to the extent that along with a new home a woman was even given a new name and identity. Once having entered her marital home it was enjoined upon her never to leave it except on a pall. And if she did dare to cross its sacrosanct portals during her lifetime, she was written off as dead for the family. Matrimony was thus an incontrovertible verdict on the woman's fate. However, by skillfully linking all the figures in the pal[l]-an-quin frame—one occupant four carriers—the poet argues that power and cruelty are the prerogatives of men. Again, the poem's studied anti-intellectualism deftly aligns the poet to the muted group without any maudlin sentimentality, thus transforming it into a powerful location of destructive male hegemonic tendencies.

What has been obliquely suggested in 'Palanquin-Bearers,' has been overtly articulated in 'Village-Song' (60), which seems a befitting sequel to the former and is quoted here, in full:

> Honey, child, honey, child, whither are you going?
> Would you cast your jewels all to the breezes blowing?
> Would you leave the mother who on golden grain has fed you?
>
> Would you grieve the lover who is riding forth to wed you?
> Mother mine, to the wild forest I am going,
> Whereupon the *champa* boughs the *champa* buds are blowing;
> To the koil-haunted river-isles where lotus lilies glisten,
> The voices of the fairy-folk are calling me, O listen!
>
> Honey, child, honey, child, the world is full of pleasure,
> Of bridal-songs and cradle-songs and sandal-scented leisure.
> Your bridal robes are in the loom, silver and saffron glowing,
> Your bridal cakes are on the hearth: O are you going?
>
> The bridal-songs and the cradle-songs have cadences of sorrow,

> The laughter of the sun today, the wind of death tomorrow.
> Far sweeter sound the forest-notes where forest-stream are falling,
> O mother mine, I cannot stay, the fairy-folk are calling.

The evocation of an exotic landscape, a dream-like idyll replete with twinkling streams, fragrant trees, singing birds and glistening flowers, however, is not just a romantic, feminine isle where the fairy-folk promise an earthly paradise. Nor is it just "an example of Sarojini's aesthetics of excess," as Paranjape puts it. (213) By exploiting rhetoric and topos developed by male poets to flatter beautiful women, the poet locates in this feminized landscape, a utopian vision. This woman-centered world with its quasi-divine presence promises life, growth and shelter from an oppressive sun, which offers light today but singes to "death tomorrow." The poem, thus, becomes a site of female meanings associated with wedlock, nurturing and maternity-institutions from which the adolescent girl wishes to break free. The escape into a dark and mysterious forest, whose ruling deities are the fairy-folk, thus imitates the ritual of beating the bounds of an unfair society with its "cadences of sorrow." This visionary forest, whose unfathomable secrets hold forth the promise of growth and renewal, runs like a leitmotif in Sarojini's poetry. Significantly the poem, which is an indictment of rigid and confining patriarchal conventions, opens with a volley of interrogatives but closes on a more decisive note. Presented in the form of a dialogue between a mother and daughter, it focuses on the two women's growing sense of alienation within mainstream life. The older woman is constrained enough not to be able to break free of a circumventing patriarchy, which she silently though unwittingly endorses. However, the poet strategically presents the daughter as a survivor and not a victim. Veering between admonition and appeasement, the mother first reminds her daughter of her social, filial and conjugal responsibilities, then tempts her with the palliative of "sandal-scented pleasure," but finally grants her tacit approval by not chiding the younger woman for choosing the pleasures of the wild forest instead.

Through this act of silent acquiescence, the poem is transformed from an innocent folk song into an immediate location of female empathy and bonding. This does not necessarily imply that Sarojini envisioned a separatist commune from which all male presence was to be banished. Her objections were only to the unequal terms of the man-woman relationship and her strategy had evolved from an acute sense of justice, from a compulsive need for universal harmony and balance.

The poem 'Suttee' (61), about the Hindu custom of a widow burning on her husband's pyre, highlights the tragedy of romanticizing misfortune, loss and martyrdom by creating such nobility and grace around it that it becomes an ideal. Although the poem is on the surface, about conjugal love and devotion, the sub-text exposes the hypocrisy of idealizing rites that help keep the oppressed in place. The sequence of ambiguous interrogatives raised at the end of each stanza reinforces the age-old adage of woman being just an insignificant portion of a larger whole. She is Adam's rib that cannot *be,* without him and therefore must die with him. Through an aesthetically appealing romanticisation of sati, Sarojini effectively subverts a custom that denies widows the right to life. Each successive stanza forcefully builds up the idea of woman's purposelessness without man, through recurring images of defenselessness that underscore the plight of widows who are confined to shadow lives of "living dark," once the "spark" and "glory" vested in their husbands has vanished. Also, by skillfully associating tropes of light, growth and life with the male, the poet links the female with him in a relationship of utter dependence and subjugation. How shall the "blossom" live when the "tree" is dead? How shall the "flesh" survive when the "soul" is gone? The poem is, thus, a frightening representation of how windows have been controlled and even programmed to accept their fate in silence. While seeming to romanticize the infamous Hindu practice of sati, the poet helps recall subtly, the damage callously done to so many women over thousands of years, through social norms that have been repeatedly reinforced in literature and have even received scriptural sanction through generations.

Love and the fleetingness of reality remained dominant concerns for Sarojini and this accounts for the perennial appeal and strength of her poetry. However, her poems cannot be submitted to chronological analysis and must be appreciated for their power to capture effectively, intense moments of experience and vision. Despite privileges and a supportive family, her poems reflect a deep sense of alienation as well as a desire for a Byzantine reality she knew was only artistically attainable. Her poems therefore were addressed to the common reader not to the specialist, for her constant endeavor was to "touch the secret poetry of every human life." Poems like 'In the Forest' (64), 'To the God of Pain' (65) and 'My Dead Dream' (66), then record the poet's profound disillusionment and pain, which are the natural concomitants of such a vision. This feeling is most evident in poems where she is not at pains to capture Indianness and exploit incidental local color or national fervor:

> For us the travail and the heat:
> The broken secrets of our pride,
> The strenuous lessons of defeat,
> The flower deferred, the fruit denied,
> But not the peace, supremely won,
> Lord Buddha, of thy Lotus-throne. (73)

Sarojini's love poems have often been lauded or criticized for their ability or lack of it, to capture love in all its variousness. Love is not an abstract ideal but alters within the varying contexts of youth, maturity, memory and religion and is at once an exciting event and a sticky business. While extolling her representation of maternal love, Elena J. Kallinnikova highlights "the freshness of feeling, filled with the joy of love which knows no bounds" (61). Chavan co-relates the poet's idea of love with "the Bhakti cult of Hindu religion . . . as externalized in Mirabai's worship of God Krishna" (24) and quotes 'The Temple,' as her "most comprehensive attempt . . . to define the nature of love and the *tensions generated by it.*" (63, my italics) However, she believes that the poet is "ambiguous in defining the exact nature of the love relationship," as she attempts to fuse Hindu, Christian and Persian modes of worship. (24) The sequence nevertheless, has received appreciation from several critics for its thematic and structural significance. A.N. Dwivedi argues that "the kind of love we find in Sarojini is inspired by the *lofty Indian ideals of self-sacrifice.*" (*IAP* 225, my italics) Likewise, L.N. Mishra supports this view and traces in her poetry the influence of "the medieval devotional poets, especially the Vaishnavites," (131) because of its color and romance. For P.V. Rajyalaxmi, "the agony of waiting, the anguish of separation and the implacable union all inherent in her 'Allegory of Love,'" are traceable not only to the Bhakti tradition of Hinduism but also to "the metaphysical idiom of the West, and the mystical *logos* of the Sufis." Finally she states: "Love becomes a waiting upon grace, and correspondingly, passion becomes a prayer. The profane circle of love vanishes into the still-center of divine being." (95) Paranjape draws attention to Sarojini's use of Indian poetic traditions, especially in her love poetry and goes on to enumerate several situations and stances—fickleness, vanity, self-indulgence, capriciousness—stereotypically associated with women in Indian poetics in the man-woman relationship. (16) It is interesting to observe how these critics have highlighted *devotion*, *worship*, *self-sacrifice* and *feminine graces*—traits that encourage and celebrate the abrogation of personality—as the dominant features of Sarojini's love poetry. While it is eminently true that these sentiments are integral to the Indian cultural psyche, they are in direct conflict with the ideals and principles of equality, more so in the context of gender relations. Lover and beloved are almost invariably locked in an unequal relationship, where woman is suppliant to the point of romantic idealization of a truant male deity, ironically recalling an inverted Petrarchanism. Sarojini's poetry cannot be viewed as a battleground for the war of the sexes, for she could never have conformed to any form of radical or militant feminism. Yet it does reflect very silently and very subtly, a deep and abiding concern for potentially intrinsic relationships that can be soured and undermined in a meaningless struggle for power. Although her biographer Padmini Sengupta reiterates that the poet had never made frank confessions of emotional disturbance to anyone (109), she does admit to the fact that she had been disappointed in the love for which she had sacrificed her all (45). This concern operates even in the poems that rely on myth and religion for poetic material. Consequently a poem like 'The Quest' (125), which is perceived as the culmination of her life-long quest for Divine love, too, is at the subtextual level a more poetic than pious poem. In this poem the poetic subject is split into self and other, I and thou, the beloved and the lover. The narrative moves from first person to second, till in an epiphanic moment the poet realizes that both selves are part of her own empirical and inner reality. From a distraught, imploring, passive beloved in vain search of an elusive lover, the poet is metamorphosed into a self-reliant woman who situates her power-source in "the nectar bubbling from my own heart's chalice." The central conflict of the poem that springs from the absence of an external guiding principle is resolved by locating that principle within her own *Brahman* or inner self. Ghanshyam (another name for Krishna) is the poetic manifestation of that power which, like Emily Dickinson, she can articulate only in masculine terms.

In his essay 'Authority and Identity in India,' the renowned critic T.G. Vaidyanathan states that unlike the sovereign Occidental self, the Indian self has no autonomous identity. He defines this self as a fluid, 'deliquescent' entity, which is reliant for its identity on an external authority. Attributing this to the difference between Western and Eastern theological beliefs, social conventions and cultural practices, he traces the central psyche in the deferential *guru-shishya* (master-disciple) tradition that "runs like a *leitmotif* through India's checkered history." (148) To illustrate this, he cites Rama the righteous hero of India's most 'beloved' epic *Ramayana*, as India's cultural hero and the guiding principle of India's cultural psyche. This he attributes to Rama's qualities of renunciation, devotion to duty and unquestioned deference to the patriarch, even to the exclusion of all other considerations including his consort Sita. However, while Rama is the ruling deity of the Indian masculine mind, Krishna with his ethics of beauty and sensuality is the preferred deity of the Indian feminine mind. Sarojini's Krishna poems can thus be seen as a celebration of the divine musician Krishna's ethics of self-reliance or *swadharma*—a key concept in the *Bhagvad Gita*—translated by the noted Indian philosopher Ananda Coomaraswami as own morality and own norm. Again, even though the poet longs for the serenity of the Buddha, her altar is reserved for the Eternal Mother of Hindu worship Kali, who is without reservation the presiding deity of her temple:

> O terrible and tender and divine!
> O mystic mother of all sacrifice . . . ,
> All gifts of life and death we bring to thee, ...
> All glory and all grace we bring to thee,
> Kali! Maheshwari. (101-2)

Through her tribute to the Goddess of consummate womanhood, the poet highlights the potential inherent in the female principle and the significant role it can play in restoring peace and harmony.

Although the question of identity for Sarojini was cultural-specific and she remained an Indian at heart, she did imbibe from the other cultures she was exposed to in the same way as historical situations create cultural consequences. This is quite evident from her special ease and intimacy with English, as well as from the fusion of Western and Eastern sensibility in her art. Indian cultural gurus would be tempted to define Sarojini as a female *trishanku* suspended between two worlds, for it is true that the claim for personal autonomy was imbibed from the Western notion of a sovereign self and was contrary to Indian notions of identity. Yet the poet's demand did break new ground in the struggle for women's autonomy and freedom, without being divorced from the cultural mainstream of her historical time and space. Although Sarojini was not an overtly political poet even in the restricted sense, her poetry and prose does register a general protest against violence—physical or emotional. It suggests a viable alternative in the power of love and spiritual awakening, even while it idealizes the worth of the individual and speaks to the heart in the language of the heart. Her work veers between ecstasy and pain but never does her faith in its power to move the human heart, give way to despair. Her lyrical songs offer:

> The solace of faith to the lips that falter,
> Succour of hope to the hands that fail
> The tidings of joy when Peace shall triumph
> When Truth shall conquer and love prevail. (88)

The enduring appeal of Sarojini's work lies in her passionate commitment to and faith in the power of love and art to affect change. Although the force of poetry to alter our attitudes is what most accounts for its effectiveness, the subtle role of ideology cannot really be denied. The context of her poetry, then, is to be traced not only in the weighty problem of national freedom, given her particular history and historical situation, but also to be located in and understood as a desire for personal and individual autonomy within the parameters of the dominant social framework.

Works Cited

Baig, Tara Ali. 1974. *Sarojini Naidu*. New Delhi: Sterling.

Chavan, Sunanda P. 1984. *The Fair Voice: A Study of Indian Women Poets in English*. New Delhi: Sterling.

Cousins, James H. 1918. *The Renaissance of India*. Madras: Ganesh.

Dwivedi, A.N. 1979. *Indo-Anglian Poetry*. Allahabad: Kitab Mahal. Hereafter cited as *IAP*.

_______. 1992. *Sarojini Naidu and Her Poetry*. Allahabad: Kitab Mahal. Hereafter cited as *SNP*.

Gosse, Edmund. 1912. 'Introduction.' *The Bird of Time: Songs of Life, Death and the Spring*. London: Heinemann.

Jain, Jasbir. Ed. 2000. *Creating Theory: Writers on Writing*. Delhi: Pencraft International.

Jussawala, Adil. *Journal of Commonwealth Literature*. No. 5. 1968. 66.

Kalinnikova, Elena J. 1982. *Indian English Literature*. Trans. V.P. Sharma. Ghaziabad: Vimal.

Khan, Izzat Yar. 1983. *Sarojini Naidu: The Poet*. New Delhi: S. Chand.

King, Bruce. Ed. 1992. *Modern Indian Poetry*. Delhi: O.U.P.

Mehrotra, A.K. Ed. 1990. *Twenty Indian Poems*. Delhi: O.U.P.

Mishra, L.N. 1995. *The Poetry of Sarojini Naidu*. Delhi: B.R.

Naidu, Sarojini. *Sarojini Naidu: Selected Poetry and Prose*, ed. with intro. Makarand Paranjape. New Delhi: Indus. 1993.

Naik, M.K. Ed. 1984. *Perspectives on Indian Poetry in English*. New Delhi: Abhinav.

Paranjape, M. Ed. Intro. 1993. *Sarojini Naidu: Selected Poetry and Prose*. New Delhi: Indus.

Rajyalakshmi, P.V. "Sarojini Naidu: Poet of Old Verities." *Perspectives on Indian Poetry in English*. 90-97.

Sarang, Vilas. Ed. Intro. 1995. *Indian English Poetry since 1950: An Anthology*. Bombay: Orient Longman

Sengupta, Padmini. 1966. *Sarojini Naidu: A Biography*. London: Asia.

Vaidyanathan. T.G. "Authority and Identity in India." *Daedalus*, 1990.

Walsh, William. 1990. *Modern Indian Poetry in English*. Delhi: O.U.P.

A Terrible Beauty: Sylvia Plath

You ask me why I spend my life writing?
Do I find entertainment?
Is it worthwhile?
Above all does it pay?
If not, then, is there a reason?
I write only because
There is a voice within me
That will not be still.

Sylvia Plath

At sixteen, Sylvia Plath wrote this poem which showed a remarkable knowledge of her own voice and destiny which, in essence, never changed. She knew she must write. Had she been alive today she would have been a venerable sixty-nine. Unfortunately, the life of this very sensitive and gifted Pulitzer Prize winning poet was rudely snuffed out, bringing to an end a promising poetic career which resulted in incalculable loss to the already growing corpus of women's writing. The winter of 1962-63 found Plath living in a small London flat—23 Fitzroy Road—with two children, ill with flu, low on money, hopelessly betrayed and tragically isolated. On Feb. 11, 1963, she gassed herself to death three months after Ted Hughes, her husband of six years, left her for another woman. Hughes maintained a studied silence amidst media frenzy generated by the tragic incident, not offering even a memoir. Seldom has a poet's death spawned so much interest and debate after death than perhaps Sylvia Plath's suicide at the young age of thirty. The latest to be included in a formidable but impressive body of scholarship and serious deliberations on the poet's life and career is *Birthday Letters*, Ted Hughes' last volume of poems before his death in October 1998. In this volume Hughes has offered: "poetic meditations on his marriage to Sylvia Plath" (Gray 1) and finally broken the puzzling and infuriating thirty-five-year silence that he had maintained on his turbulent courtship and equally stormy marriage to the outwardly exuberant but inwardly disturbed Plath. He had first met her in February 1956 while studying in Pembroke College, Cambridge, in "A picture of that year's intake of Fulbright Scholars" (*BL* 3) and had married her in June the same year. Few in England had heard of this American expatriate before her death, but with the posthumous publication of *Ariel (*1956), by her husband and literary executor Hughes, the Plath legend was born. It is little wonder then, that *Birthday Letters* has made front-page headlines on both sides of the Atlantic. The furore over the book, however, is not difficult to be traced to reasons beyond the realm of aesthetic appreciation. The book cannot really be defined as the summit of the erstwhile British poet Laureate's achievement. One stands in agreement with Keith Sagar that to do so would be "as absurd as it would be to claim that the sonnets (revelatory as they are) are the pinnacle of Shakespeare's" entire oeuvre.

Birthday Letters is premised on two key contentions that Hughes states quite early in the volume. The first is that the electra-complexed Plath was destined to kill herself and the second, that Hughes was powerless before her "dybbuk fury" (144) and her "Germanic scowl," which "would not translate itself" (143). He writes that Plath's "Daddy" was her "god with the smoking gun" (17), her "Ogre lover" (159), who had embedded "sleepless electrodes" (142) into her temples so that in each night's sleep she "descended" into her "father's grave" and each night:

> I hypnotized calm into you,
> Courage, understanding and calm,

Nevertheless it was hardly of any help, for:

> Each night you descended again
> Into the temple-crypt,

That private, primal cave
Under the public dome of father-worship. (141)

In poem after poem, he underscores Plath's obsession with her father and her "doomed," "tortured, crying/suffocating self," locked:

Into some chamber gasping for oxygen
Where I could not find you, or really hear you,
Let alone understand you. (146)

'Fairy Tale' (159-61) is another poem in which Hughes gives a scathing account of Plath's father-fixation. He claims to have had access to forty-eight chambers of Plath's life but "forty-nine was [her] magic number," the inaccessible secret chamber to which she kept the keys. When he managed to unlock it by means of the skeleton key of a blade of grass, he discovered that it was her father's "abyss" into which she descended each night and into which, he too had been involuntarily sucked up:

As I tripped
Over your corpse and fell with him
Into his abyss.

Her father was 'The Bee God' that Hughes mentions in the volume:

When you wanted bees I never dreamed
It meant your Daddy had come up out of the well. (150)

and like a "lone bee" had:

Soared over the housetop and down
And locked onto my brow. (152)

When he first met her he says he did not know that he:

was being auditioned
For the male lead in your drama, . . .
As if a puppet were being tied on its strings. (7)

Feminists have cried foul. It is indeed difficult to believe Hughes' claim that in Plath's life he was just "an accompaniment carrying babies," "waiting," for her to "come back to nature" (144), trailing "after her like a dog." (145) On the contrary, *The Unabridged Journals of Sylvia Plath*, which contain all but the last two journals written during the last three years of her life, have a devastating story to tell. Edited by Karen V. Kukil, these journals have been restored from the heavily edited version authorized and made public by Hughes in 1982 and reflect a more slavish devotion to Hughes. They stand testimony to the ways in which she relied on him to define herself and are a stark indictment of Hughes' emotional and sexual defection and subsequent desertion. Also, as Carole Maso states, the "restored material conveys on nearly every page the *pressures convention placed* on her head, the intricate dynamics of her relationships, and the degrees to which she relied on her work to make her, in the most direct and urgent way *real*." (Emphasis added 1)

Even though self-justification is a legitimate aim of poetry, Ted Hughes' maudlin my-side-of-the-story book of poems in which he insists he was just "a fly outside on the window-pane/ of my own domestic drama" (145) then, seems to ring false. Furthermore, the fact that Assia, the woman he left Plath for, and their daughter Shura, had also gassed themselves to death in a macabre deja vu, does little to support Hughes' self-justification.

To assess Plath's poems as the pathologically disordered, though clear out-pouring of a father-obsessed and death-infatuated artist, would be doing great disservice to her work, which might have reached even greater heights of imaginative enlargement had she lived longer. Throughout the decades following her death, Plath's work has continued to gain considerable following, even a cult of impassioned believers and commentators, who swear by St. Sylvia the high priestess of suffering. Her works help us understand better, the gap between how she acted and how she felt. They provide us with startling insights into how practiced she was like most women, in the art of subterfuge, role playing and dissimulation "for the thrill" (*CP* 228), so as to deny even essential aspects of her own psyche. As such Plath's posthumous volume *Ariel*, the bleak, violent and beautiful book of poems written in the months before her death, assumes crucial significance in light of the complex nature of the relationship between the poet's troubled life and her brilliant work. The book was written during the downward spin, which brought her to her suicide. During the months following her separation, the hardness of her life seemed to increase her need to write. Working furiously and with a sense of urgency during the wee hours of the day before the children woke up, she would sometimes finish a poem a day. In these last poems it is as if some deeper, more powerful demonic energy had grabbed control, giving death a cruel physical allure and making psychic pain almost tactile. The poems of this volume seem like smoldering volcanoes ready to erupt and convey powerfully the sense of dormant pressure under which the poet lived her life. Her mother's "wishes/Hiss at [her] sins" (*CP* 226), the "potatoes hiss" in the kitchen (*CP* 227), in fact the whole "room is a hiss" (*CP* 203). Anthony Thwaite rightly suggests that "most of her poems are wisps of smoke above a cone, indicating but not embodying the violence below" (62), like a battle between the expression and submergence of rage. It is eminently true that there are several celebratory poems that are lit with Plath's unique excitement and capture imaginatively the quality of felt life and her sensuous apprehension of the world. Yet, it is also true that there are a larger number of poems in the corpus of her work—*The Colossus* (1960), *Ariel* (1965), *Crossing the Water* (1971) and *Winter Trees* (1971)—all brought together in *Collected Poems* (1982), that are to the contrary. These poems, which also include a section of uncollected 'Juvenilia' composed before 1956, are dominated by a strong sense of the psychic split that the poet experienced during her short but intensely lived life. Some of the grave personal discontinuities which underlay a surface perfection, doubtless had their origin in the death of her father, a college professor and an expert on bees, when Plath was just a child of eight. As she had once confided to Nancy Steiner her friend and roommate at Smith College, the memory of her father invariably evoked ambivalent feelings in her. "He was an autocrat," she said. "I adored him and despised him, and I probably wished many times that he were dead. When he obliged me and died, I imagined that I had killed him" (Steiner 10). Through a complex process of introjection then, she had lived with her father's ghost, which was to haunt her throughout her life. That her fierce love for him always superseded her powerful utterances of hatred however—"Daddy, daddy, you bastard, I'm through" (*CP* 224)—is indisputable. She could never really recover fully from the emotional loss of "the black man who/Bit my pretty red heart in two" (*CP* 224). "Panzer-man" Otto Plath's ominous shadow hovers in her poems like a ubiquitous presence. He is the colossus she could never "never get . . . put together entirely," the sepulchral creature of the netherworld whose "arms" arched towards her "out of death" (*BL* 160), beckoning her to join him. Nevertheless, it is important to remember that Plath's work was vitally linked to the totality of her life and experience and it is possible therefore, to discover other more disturbing and compelling reasons for her psychic split besides her obsession with the early and irreparable loss of a parent.

Born on October 27, 1932 to Otto and Aurelia Plath—a middle-class, intellectual, German-speaking couple—in Jamaica Plain, Massachusetts, Sylvia Plath had shown early poetic promise by publishing her first poem in the *Boston Sunday Herald* at eight years. The poem reflects not only the little girl's keen observation and poetic propensities, which were not to be ignored, but also holds forth in its simple, childish utterance, the hope of better things to come:

> Hear the crickets chirping
> In the dewy grass.
> Bright little fireflies
> Twinkle in the grass. (Qtd. Aird 5)

The poet's interest in writing was greatly encouraged by Mr. Crockett, her English teacher at Bradford High School and as she confessed in a long unpublished poem, the urge in her to write, was compulsive:

> There is a voice within me
> That will not be still. (*LH* 35)

Sensitive, intelligent, passionately ambitious and compelled towards perfection in everything she attempted, Plath's poetic drive had ultimately subsumed all other roles in the grand role of the artist, even though her mother, in keeping with the cultural conventions of her time, had other plans for her. She was on the surface a model daughter, popular in school, earning straight A's, winning the best prizes, but as she admits in 'The Disquieting Muses':

> I learned, I learned, I learned elsewhere,
> From muses unhired by you, dear mother. (*CP* 75)

By the time she entered Smith College, Northampton, on a scholarship from Olive Higgins Prouty, she already had an impressive list of publications to which she added over four hundred poems while at Smith. During the summer following her junior year at college, Plath had nearly succeeded in killing herself with an overdose of sleeping pills after her return from New York City, where she had been a 'guest editor' for *Mademoiselle* magazine. She later described this experience vividly, in her autobiographical novel, *The Bell Jar* (1963). After a period of recovery involving electroshock and psychotherapy, she resumed her pursuit of academic excellence and literary success, graduated from Smith *summa cum laude* and won a Fulbright Scholarship to Cambridge, England.

Plath's compulsive need for approval and success was further complicated by a terrifying dread of otherness, which she saw as separation and this could perhaps be one of the dominant reasons for her psychic discontinuities. She recalls that she first encountered this feeling as a two-and-a-half-year-old at her grandparents' home at Nauset, just after her brother Warren was born. In 'Ocean 1212-W,' which appeared in *The Listener* in

1963 and forms a relief map of her childhood landscape, she recalls how she "hated babies." She: "who for two and a half years had been the center of a tender universe felt the axis wrench." From being center stage she was now being reduced to a mere "bystander." She recalls how "her beautiful fusion with the things of the world was over," once she became aware of the "separateness of everything." (*JP* 23) The birth of another child meant fear of separation, of being rejected by the mother and for Plath the only way to life was through fusion, through the consequent erasure of a separate self. This was just the kind of life women were supposed to draw from marriage, motherhood, men. Hence a life without fusion, without the unequivocal approval of her mother was no life at all. To fulfill in every way the narcissistic expectations of her mother—and had her father been alive his too perhaps—in order to maintain this fusion, therefore became an overwhelming need. After her father's death her mother, an ambitious and accomplished woman in her own right, had suppressed and abandoned her own dreams and desires without wincing. Also, Aurelia Plath had denied her children access to any feelings of regret and rage she might have felt at having to adopt the life of drudgery that she had been confined to, by force of circumstances. Her constant endeavor was to present to her children a picture of fortitude and strength that lay in the "made to order stories" where "Mixie Blackshort" was "the heroic bear" and the "witches, always, always/ got baked into gingerbread." (*CP* 75) The reason for this too, could perhaps be found in Aurelia Plath's own deep need to fuse and to see only good in everything. As a topos of self-denying love and affection, Aurelia Plath had thus unwittingly become not only her daughter's role model but also her oppressor, by forcing her into as unauthentic a life as she herself had lived. To gain popularity then, became part of Sylvia Plath's larger strategy of success and as she admits self-mockingly, she became "a pathological liar." (*CP* 227) Overtaken by an obsessive need to reward her mother for the "life blood and care" (*LH* 113) that she had expended rearing Warren and her, the young girl's terror at not being able to became as relentless as the older woman's "abnormally altruistic tendencies." (*LH* 112) Plath was thus torn between the contrary pulls of her own vital self and her filial obligations and her fractured psyche struggled to find a viable identity that would restore balance in her life. As Adrienne Rich significantly observes, the poet's compulsions "to lay in her mother's lap . . . poems and prizes, books and babies," (*OWB* 230) is the single most compulsive theme of *Letters Home*. Aurelia Plath had unknowingly caused a split between what her daughter wanted to be and what she had forced herself to become, in her attempts to repay a debt of gratitude. The poet's resentment against a mother who had pushed her into this life of dissimulation and subterfuge and who she felt had used her as "an extension of herself" (*J* 281), then comes across sharply in poems like 'The Disquieting Muses' (74-76), and 'Medusa' (224-26). In 'The Disquieting Muses,' she rebukes the mother for feeding her on a factious reality that "bobbed away/like a soap-bubble." But her rage against the crippling Medusan presence of her "Old barnacled umbilicus," which kept itself "in a state of miraculous repair," comes across with even greater umbrage in 'Medusa':

> In any case, you are always there,
> Tremulous breath at the end of my line,
> Curve of water upleaping
> To my water rod, dazzling and grateful
> Touching and sucking.
>
> I didn't call you
> I didn't call at all.
> Nevertheless, nevertheless
> You steamed to me over the sea,
> Fat and red, a placenta
>
> Paralyzing the kicking lovers.

She desperately tries to shake "off, off" her "eely tentacle" and declares indignantly:

There is nothing between us.

Like every woman living in the U.S. in mid-twentieth century, both Aurelia and Sylvia Plath identified success as a woman with a successful marriage, even if it entailed a subsumption of female identity. Personal ambition, autonomy and otherness were discordant with conventional feminine behavior and were identified with bitterness, self-doubt, hatred, rage and self-destruction. The social psychologist and founder of second-wave feminism Betty Friedan points out, that after the feminist gains of the early twentieth century she detected a concerted campaign since the end of World War II, to convince American women that they could achieve happiness in life only through marriage and motherhood. Her book *The Feminine Mystique,* was the first ingenious research and investigation into the social and cultural construction of femininity in the U.S in mid-twentieth century. In it she suggests that this ideology served several social needs and reflected an impact on women's opportunities in the 1950s, which found middle-class women back in the home. "Fulfillment as a woman had only one definition . . . the housewife-mother," she wrote. Contentment for women lay in "sexual passivity, male domination and nurturing maternal love." (37) Significantly, mid-twentieth century women had not moved much beyond their nineteenth century counterparts and like Jane Austen's women, they too were nurtured on and for passivity. Victorian culture did not permit women to accept or gratify their basic sexual needs, but mid-twentieth century culture did not permit them: "to accept or gratify their basic need to grow and fulfill themselves as women." (Schnelr 49) As Paula Bennett significantly points out, if "in Emily Dickinson's time a woman's success was . . . measured in terms of *usefulness*," both at home and in society, "a hundred years later changes in American society had shrunk this narrow horizon to an even more narrow goal." (101) The values of nurture now were that the purpose of life is personal success earned by hard work and measured in fame and money. The fragile foundation, on which Plath was encouraged to build her sense of identity and self-worth then, took on the profile of a successful marriage and efficient housewifery, with back breaking domesticity as its natural concomitant. Consequently, the desire for personal fame and money got subsumed by a "willingness to accept second place in the market of ideas." (Bennett 116) She became Aurelia Plath's very superior daughter who had married an even more superior male just as her mother had done before her and was transformed into 'the plastic wife of *Letters Home* the sweet, submissive, self-sacrificing and courageous girl who clipped recipes from the *Ladies' Home Journal*." (Bennett 114) Ostensibly, she loved to "cook and make a house, and surge force into a man's dreams," as she wrote in her *Journals.* (109) When Ted Hughes' first volume of poems, *The Hawk in the Rain* was accepted for publication she wrote: "I am more happy than if it was my first book published. I have worked so closely on these poems of Ted's and typed them so many countless times through revision after revision that I feel ecstatic about it all. I am so happy his book is accepted first." (*LH* 297)

Ironically enough, like several women before her including Aurelia Plath, Sylvia Plath's inputs in terms of the secretarial assistance she had rendered to Hughes in the production of his book, went unrecognized and unreckoned as work, for in economic parlance only paid work constitutes production. She had learnt to accept quietly this fact that gives a fascinating look into the dynamics of female oppression.

If Plath craved for the unfaltering approval of her mother, her need for the unconditional love and approval of her husband was even greater. She could therefore not take full hold of the freedom Hughes' desertion actually offered her. She probably perceived her break-up with him as having failed both, her mother and her husband and this could possibly have led to the final suicidal depression. The final separation from Hughes had unleashed in her the demons that had lain suppressed and dormant for so long and had haunted her since Nauset. Plath was thus metamorphosed from a good, sweet girl who "dried plates with [her] dense hair" (*CP* 214), into the flame-haired 'Lady Lazarus' who ate "men like air" (*CP* 247).

Apart from the strong formative influence Plath's mother wielded on her notions of identity, social success and expectations, there were several other cultural pressures that worked on her as on other women, during her time. A host of media-evoked, romanticized versions of gender relations in the Fifties, functioned subliminally to emphasize that a woman's proper place was at home minding the kids. Bennett emphasizes more particularly, the vital role psychologists played in reinforcing surreptitiously, such falsehoods about women. She quotes a telling passage from Peter Blos's book *On Adolescence: A Psychoanalytical Interpretation*, in which Blos infers that it is "the prerogative of the female to display her physical charms" and to "emphasize and enhance it through the use of cosmetics, adornments and dress. Her need is to be loved." (102) This she believes "epitomize[d] the thinking that family experts in this period foisted as truth upon women." (102) Blos's comments were, quite obviously, a conscious attempt to subvert all previous gains that women had garnered for themselves, by foisting on them an intentional passivity. It is little wonder then, that a woman who went to college between 1945 and 1960: "could hardly avoid learning . . . not to get interested in anything besides having children if she wanted to be *normal, happy, and adjusted, feminine*." (Friedan 148, my italics) In ironic replication of Mary Lyon's America in the nineteenth century, power, authority, action and personal success were bastions reserved for males. Thus, unlike Dickinson who chose a life outside domesticity and wedlock, Plath seems to have accepted that the only way she could find herself complete as a woman was through marriage and motherhood, even though this ideology seemed to run contrary to her own independent, vibrant and ambitious nature. Also unlike Dickinson, for Plath the writing of great poetry alone could never be enough. A common theme throughout her writing was the intense desire to be a loving wife and mother, as long as she could still speak from within her "deeper self" through her writing. "I will write till I begin to speak my deep self and then have children and speak still deeper," she wrote in her *Journals* (166). It is then no accident, when she says:

> The blood jet is poetry
> There is no stopping it. (*CP* 270)

She saw the creation of poetry and the creation of babies as mutually enriching just as she linked success as a woman to success as a wife. Believing that it was possible to combine the erotic and the intellectual she wrote: "I would live a life of conflict, of balancing children, sonnets, love and dirty dishes." (*J* 126) Till the last year of her life she seemed to have sincerely believed that marriage and motherhood were the only means to success, no matter how hazardous they may be to her as a poet.

One precondition to marriage that Plath had voiced in her *Journals* was that she would not be bound by the man she married into becoming a woman she did not want to be: "I must find a strong, potential, powerful mate who can counter my vibrant, dynamic self: sexual and intelligent and while comradely, I must admire him: respect and admiration must equate with the object of my love." (*J* 13) In her dreams of the future, Plath had envisioned an ideal mate but had never entertained any delusion that a mate could take place either of her ravenous muse, or any part of a full life. Neither did she want to be "Christ-like" as Keith Sagar rightly suggests. "She wanted fulfillment" (80). Unfortunately, her inability to find a solution to the conflict between the "needs of gender and the requirements of genre" as Bennett puts it, was what finally destroyed her. When she first met Ted Hughes she felt she had found her equal, the man worthy of her complete devotion, the only mate worthy of her body and soul, of her talent and ambition, the man with whom life would be ideal. The relationship sadly enough, turned sour only too soon:

> Tight wires between us,
> Pegs too deep to uproot, and a mind like a ring

> Sliding shut on some quick thing,
> The constriction killing me also. (*CP* 194)

Hughes' betrayal and subsequent desertion therefore, had left her completely devastated and she could never really recover from the blow. While he lost both, her respect and her admiration, she lost love along with her dreams of an ideal future. During the bleak days following her break-up with Hughes, poetry offered the only refuge and to this she turned with unbridled frenzy, releasing poetic energies that were to finally consume her.

The pain, frustration and bitterness of her lost and last years erupt violently in fits of uncontrolled rage in the poems of *Ariel*, which tellingly capture that unique voice of her own "deep self." Understandably then, these poems reflect a strong streak of misandry, which takes on the form of a hysterical hatred for sex despite her sensual nature, especially in the poems written after her separation. A story that had started out just right—the coming together of two intense, brilliant and ambitious poets—had spiraled off into the realm of Greek tragedy in which even their two children, Frieda Rebecca and Nick, had become a marginal presence. A teetering marriage juxtaposed with Hughes' infidelities and professional jealousies and her own, prickly and provocative personality, resulted in tearing asunder a relationship that was even otherwise under continual siege. A messy personal life was the hydra-headed monster that led her to the bottom of her board of snakes and ladders. Man and marriage were, thus, vociferously denounced:

> Attendants!
> And at his next step
> I shall unloose
>
> I shall unloose—
> From the small jeweled
> Doll he guards like a heart—
>
> The lioness,
> The shriek in the bath,

The cloak of holes. (*CP* 243-44)

Written just months before her death, Plath's poem, 'Purdah' (*CP* 242-44) imagines the world of a woman completely under patriarchal control. However, under a surface calm in which the woman awaits her "bridegroom," she is a lioness seething with rage and plotting her revenge: "like the murderous Clytemnestra of Greek classical tragedy, who stabbed her husband, Agamemnon in the bath." (Schneir 34) Yet another poem 'Aerialist,' voices the poet's desire to break free from the confines of a marriage that had reached a stalemate and is hopelessly deadlocked:

Each night, this adroit young lady
Lies among the sheets
Shredded fine as snowflakes
Until dream takes her body
From bed to strict tryouts
In tightrope acrobatics. (*CP* 331)

Man and marriage are now seen as "aspects of the menace that life poses," (Maini 182) a life in which:

nothing changes, for all the blazing of
our drastic jargons, but the clock hands that move implacably from
twelve to one. (*CP* 329)

The radiant wife who had written to her mother on Oct. 8, 1956 that she wanted, "to be the strongest paean yet for the creative forces of nature, the joy of being a loved and loving woman," has now lost her song:

I am your opus
I am your valuable,
The pure gold baby
That melts to a shriek. (*CP* 226)

In poems like 'The Jailer' (*CP* 226-27), and 'Lesbos' (*CP* 227-30), Plath vents her angst against her oppressor, her domesticity and her motherhood as well. Caught in the vice-like grip of a double life, she hisses out her rage against the diet of "lies and smiles" and the falsehoods that she has been constrained to follow:

> All day gluing my church of burnt matchsticks
> I dream of someone else entirely,
> And he for his subversion,
> Hurts me, he
> With his armor of fakery,
> His high cold mask of amnesia. (*CP* 227)

'The Jailer,' opens with a strident accusation:

> My night sweats grease his breakfast plate. . . .
> Is that all he can come up with
> The rattle of keys?

Having been continually "drugged and raped," rape becomes a paradigm for all forms of oppression. She "wishes him dead or away," but knows "That . . . is the impossibility." Realizing the brittle stuff wishes are made of, she can then only imagine him "Impotent as distant thunder." What she can do, however, is take violent action so that the poem now advances from mere wish fulfillment towards dramatic action. This sudden turn closes the poem on a more confident note. An epiphanic moment helps her realize that the oppressor is entirely dependent on her for indulging his sadistic pleasures. This awareness fills her with the breathless excitement of a new sense of power and freedom in which captive now becomes controller:

> What would the dark
> Do without fevers to eat?
> What would the light
> Do without eyes to knife, what would
> He
> Do, do, do without me?

The repeated emphasis on "do[ing]," as well as "do[ing] without," indicates the speaker's determination to shrug off a silent and debilitating submission for loud and defiant action. She knows now that she can survive very well without him, as she confidently states in a later poem:

> All by myself I am a huge camellia
> Glowing and coming and going, flush on flush. (*CP* 232)

'Lesbos,' opens with an outburst against "viciousness in the kitchen," where even "The potatoes hiss." The poem is as much an attack on marriage and domesticity as it is on its concomitant darkness, deceit and artificiality:

> It is all Hollywood, windowless,
> The fluorescent light wincing on and off like a terrible
> migraine.

Veering between anxiety for a vulnerable child and disgust at the "stink of fat and baby crap," the poet feels "doped and thick from my last sleeping pill," from the "smog of cooking, the smog of hell" and from the pressures of her "mulatto" life. Sick of play-acting loving wife and mother which, she sadly admits, she did "for the thrill," she now vents her anger against an "impotent husband" and the "acid baths" he has forced her to take. The poem marks the protagonist's significant progression from helpless forbearance to seething rage. She is done with her domesticity and subjugation and now stands "Hard and apart and white," more determined than ever before to make it alone:

> Now I am silent, hate
> Up to my neck,
> Thick, thick.
> I do not speak,
> I am packing the hard potatoes like good clothes,
> I am packing the babies
> I am packing the sick cats.

Although like the previous poem, 'Lesbos' too conveys a sense of silent determined action, it marks a progression in that it takes the protagonist further into the physical and emotional act of actually moving away, of doing without, of leaving behind. Having put away all that she no longer requires, she is now ready to make new beginnings. The process of renewal has been set in motion. Recalling the forced diet of "Lies and smiles," the poet now throws it back at its chef in a parting gesture of open defiance:

> I say I may be back,
> You know what lies are for.

The poem thus closes with Plath's terse, bitter and final farewell:

> Even in your Zen heaven we shan't meet.

'The Jailer,' and 'Lesbos,' like the volume at large, have powerful sub-texts and are both, angry poems. Not only are they power-packed articulations of the poet's conflicting selves but are also, more importantly, a demand for personal and artistic autonomy. While rape and resentment against the other come across sharply, the determination to be away and done with it, to shut the door on an inglorious chapter and to begin anew is even more forcefully conveyed. Anger thus invests the poet with a terrible power and beauty. "The little toy wife" (*CP* 233), the angel in the house eulogized for her unflinching maternal and spousal commitment, is dead. No more an epitome of self-denying love and affection, she states emphatically:

> O sister, mother, wife
> Sweet Lethe is my life.
> I am never, never, never coming home. (*CP* 233)

She is now the eternal woman:

> a pure acetylene
> Virgin
> Attended by roses
>
> By kisses, by cherubim,
> By whatever these pure things mean.
> Not you, nor him
>
> Not him (my selves dissolving old whore petticoats)—
> To paradise. (*CP* 232)

Having done with domesticity and marriage the poet is now ready to settle her score with god and man:

> Herr God, her Lucifer
> Beware,
> Beware. (*CP* 246)

The poems now flow out in their misogamic rage, against the very institution of marriage as an entrapment that promises nothing but "A ring of gold with the sun in it" and a pack of "Lies, lies and grief." (*CP* 247)

Plath's intense black hatred now pours forth as invective and scathing indictment, in stormy poems that begin to assume hallucinatory proportions even while maintaining their artistic skill and control. All veiling strategies are now stripped off in a desperate need to reveal her most dangerous secrets even at the cost of her most vital interests, even at the cost of her life. Rage and anger become her weapons against bondage and the angrier she is, the closer she gets to re-defining herself as a woman. Her poetry is now charged with a fiery energy that helps dispel enervating states. The awareness of suppression and betrayal triggers off deliberations on and a reassessment of her life hitherto and of "two kinds of fire—the fires of hell which merely agonize and the fires of heaven which purify." This is seen as a process of burning away the false self and a rebirth of the true self as Plath elucidated while introducing 'Fever 103°,' in a BBC reading of the poem. "During the poem the first sort of fire suffers itself into the second" she explained (*CP* 293). Instead of paralyzing then, rage becomes her source of empowerment. Out of the ashes of her false self, Plath the authentic woman and poet rises Phoenix-like to reclaim her world. In a reading of 'Lady Lazarus' (*CP* 244-47) prepared for BBC radio, Plath had introduced the poem saying, "The speaker is a woman who has the great and terrible gift of being reborn. The only trouble is, she has to die first. She is the Phoenix, the libertarian spirit, what you will. She is also just a good, plain, very resourceful woman." (*CP* 294) This comment forms a befitting analogue to the whole drama of her life that was enacted almost strictly, against the background of this premise. The poet who wrote and the woman who suffered were thus fused into one persona. Although rage had become a source and resource for self-definition sadly enough, in her moment of maximum rage God's rampaging lioness drove herself over the edge. So sinister was the drive towards self-definition and perfection that the poet could even visualize with cold calculation, the event of her own death in 'Edge' (*CP* 272-73) the last poem she wrote just days before the fatal tragedy:

> The woman is perfected,
> Her dead
>
> Body wears the smile of accomplishment,
> The illusion of a Greek necessity
>
> Flows in the scrolls of her toga,
> Her bare
>
> Feet seem to be saying
> We have come so far, it is over.

In an effort to overcome the double bind that women writers were caught in, Plath had to make a conscious choice between the conventional role of a woman and a rebel poet. As she stated overtly in her poem 'Female Author,' which is a comment on the role of the woman writer: "All day she plays at chess with the bones of the world." (*CP* 301) The conflict that Plath experienced between her personal values and the larger social practices and cultural assumptions that prevented her from making contact with her own self, could never be successfully resolved. The weight of an entire cultural tradition that had relegated and marginalised women, was too great to be either borne or cast off so that a poem like "Doom of Exiles" (*CP* 318), comes to be seen as an agonized admission of the futility of it all:

> Backward we travel to reclaim the day
> Before we fell, like Icarus, undone;
> All we find are altars in decay

And profane words scrawled black against the sun.

> Still stubbornly we try to crack the nut
> In which the riddle of our race is shut.

Tragedy then, as Joyce Carol Oates puts it, was "not a woman, however gifted, dragging her shadow around in a circle on analyzing with dazzling scrupulosity the stale, boring inertia of the circle." Tragedy was "culturally, mysteriously enlarging the individual so that what he has experienced is both what we have experienced and what we need not experience—because of his or her private agony." (1) Having realized the futility of words to assuage her suffering, Plath began to move grimly towards the last act of the human drama hoping to achieve through that one last daring act—the tightrope walker's fatal plunge into the unknown—what she had failed to achieve through words. Her obsession with suicide and death could be seen then, as a literal enactment of the process of renewal and rebirth. As Ted Hughes wrote in a poem significantly entitled 'Suttee':

> In the myth of your first death our deity
> Was yourself resurrected.
> Yourself reborn. The holy one. (*BL* 147)

The purpose of all serious poetry is to find a shape and meaning to the chaos of experience. For the whole length of her career, Plath had made many attempts to find suitable myths that would embody recurring experience and place her own life in its context. In this context, Keith Sagar suggests: "The two myths that came to obsess Plath were those of Phaeton and Icarus." (79) If Phaeton rode his father's chariot recklessly into darkness and oblivion, Icarus burnt his waxen wings in his ambitious flight, only to be plunged headlong into the sea. In the light of Sagar's contention then, two poems that are central to our understanding of *Ariel* are the title poem of the volume and 'Sheep in Fog' written a fortnight before her death. The equestrian trope in both poems recalls Robert Lowell's comments in his forward to the volume, that in these poems Plath is "like a racehorse galloping relentlessly with risked outstretched neck death hurdle after hurdle topped. She cries out for the rapid life of starting pistols, snapping tapes and new world records broken."

'Ariel' (*CP* 239-40) opens at a moment of 'stasis,' of suspension in darkness before the leap into kinesis. In a sudden upsurge of energy, "God's Lioness" has set out on an exhilarating and reckless ride across the "substanceless blue," leaving behind an inhibiting and enervating life. Through a gradual build up of motion and speed, the poet fuses rider and mount in an image that blurs the distinction between the rider and horse, the dancer and the dance and between the agent, the act and the object. Things fly past like "shadows" and "something else/hauls" the poet "through air." She is hurtled through space on animal power that pulls her out of her own identity into a fusion with itself. Reduced to its psychological content, the poem expresses a death wish in which the false self gets subsumed in a pure form of astral energy:

> And I am the arrow,
> The dew that flies
> Suicidal, at one with the drive
> Into the red
>
> Eye, the cauldron of morning

"Like most visionary experience in which the protagonist is invaded by divine power, the flight into the sun constitutes the consummation of being as well as a destruction." (Mckay 55) The poem thus draws an analogy with Phaeton's exhilarating but reckless drive through the heavens in his father Apollo's chariot. Losing control of the horses, Phaeton had unfortunately fallen headlong into an untimely and tragic death like a shooting star, which marks the heavens with its brightness even as it falls.

'Sheep in Fog' (*CP* 262), on the other hand, is a disturbingly bleak poem. While introducing the poem in a reading for the radio Plath had said, "In this poem, the speaker's horse is proceeding at a slow, cold walk down a hill of macadam to the stables at the bottom. It is December. It is foggy. In the fog there are sheep" (*CP* 295). The poem begins on a subdued note and marks a sharp contrast between the fiery energy of 'Ariel' and the poet's dreary chilling ride through the still darkness now. Ariel's soaring flight into the red eye of the sun has been arrested. His chariot has run off course. His spirited gallop across the skies has now becomes a slow, tortuous trot toward Hades:

> To a heaven
> Starless and fatherless, a dark water

from which, no one ever returns. Phaeton and Icarus are thus brought together in a searing image of collapse and destruction. The dominant hue of the poem is 'dark,' the movement that of a tired pilgrim dragging himself through the last lap of his troubled journey and the tone one of utter dejection. As Judith Kroll suggests in her book *Chapters in a Mythology: The Poetry of Sylvia Plath*: "before her death Sylvia Plath passed beyond the conception of mystic rebirth which had mattered to her before." (Qtd. Miller 3) The poems written in 1963, just days before her death, are thus pervaded by a deep sense of inanition and failure. It seems relevant then, to quote here, Darwin's account of Icarus' death, as a befitting analogue to Plath's final fate:

> With melting wax and loosened strings
> Sunk helpless Icarus on unfaithful wings. (Qtd. Bulfinch 195)

The twin myths of Phaeton and Icarus seemed to have narrowed Plath's fate into a choice between "a 'triumphant' death by fire or a defeated death by water." (Sagar 83) Also in line with this argument is Ted Hughes' contention: "As an image of her Ariel flight in the chariot of the God of poetry which was also her attempt to soar [plunge] into the inspirational form of her inaccessible father, to convert her former physical suicide into a psychic rebirth, that myth is the parable of the book *Ariel* and of her life and death." (Qtd. Sagar 83) However, in giving such an explanation Hughes has once again traced the source of Plath's recklessness to her desire to merge with the spirit of her dead father and absolved himself in the process, of all blame. Hughes was, in fact, as much to blame for Plath's tragic end, as were her father's ghost and her mother's tenacious, inescapable, Medusan presence. The influence of Hughes on Plath is legendary. He was one of the poets she admired most besides Blake, Yeats and Robert Lowell. Plath and Hughes had both been searching for adequate controls for the poetic energies they sought to release. Whereas in Plath's case the search was compounded and even complicated by her intensely passionate nature and she was finally consumed by her poetic energies, Hughes was a disciplined poet and had evolved his own methods of controlling the energies he had invoked. He had tried to explain Plath's tragedy by distinguishing between a "purposive and positive" upper level and a "negative and tragic" lower level at which Plath's ritual of transcendence worked. Acknowledging that at the upper level: "her shaping will [was] in control, where the ritual magic [was] choreographed according to plan and the rebirth hopeful," he states that at the lower level: "her material remained inaccessible to manipulation." (Qtd. Fenton 7) It seems quite plausible then, that the marvelous poetry of the end of her days came of a second severance from the divine male. Plath's inability to contain and control the poetic energies she had invoked at the high point of her tragic isolation and emotional despair and her inability to "manipulate" her emotions, was what finally drove her to destruction.

In 1957, Plath had written: "All I need to do is work, break open the deep mines of experience and imagination, let the words come and speak it all, sounding themselves and tasting themselves." (*J* 162) Sadly enough, she was to write just days before she took her life, that words could only offer paper consolation. They could not change the fate of star-crossed lives:

> Words dry and riderless,
> The indefatigable hoof-taps.
> While from the bottom of the pool, fixed stars
> Govern a life. (*CP* 270)

She had come to learn that there were other larger and inexplicable forces at play, that shaped human destiny. There was no God who appeared at the end of her tribulations to explain things or dispense justice, no God to reassure her that she had passed the test and now all would be well. Plath's demons had outlived her and like Yeats, she could "subdue life only to her art and not to her necessities." (Maini 185) Her cultural significance thus, lies in diagnosing through her poetry "the pathological aspects of our era that make death of the spirit inevitable." (Oates 1) Having lived her life on the edge, Plath has left behind verse of such terrible daring and near-perfect beauty that questions the very foundations of patriarchal assumptions, that even though the poetic voice has been stilled, it continues to haunt us across continents.

Works Cited

Aird, E.M. 1973. *Sylvia Plath: Her Life and Her Work*. New York: Barnes and Noble.

Bennett, Paula. 1986. *My Life a Loaded Gun: Female Creativity and Feminist Poetics*. Boston: Beacon Press.

Blos, Peter. 1962. *On Adolescence: A Psychoanalytic Interpretation*. New York: The Free Press of Glencoe.

Bullfinch, Thomas. 1993. *The Golden Age of Myth and Legend*. Hertfordshire: Wordsworth.

Fenton, James. "A Family Romance: *Birthday Letters*." *The New York Review*. Mar. 5. 1998. 7-9.

Friedan, Betty. 1974. *The Feminine Mystique*. New York: W.W. Norton and Co.

Gary, Paul. "Breaking the Silence." *Time*. Mar. 2, 1998. Vol. 151, no. 9.

Hughes, Ted. 1998. *Birthday Letters*. New York: Farrar, Straus and Giroux.

Kroll, Judith. 1976. *Chapters in a Mythology: The Poetry of Sylvia Plath*. New York: Harper and Row.

Kukil, Karen V. Ed. 2000. *The Unabridged Journals of Sylvia Plath*. New York: Anchor Books.

Maini, D.S. 1998. *The Spirit of American Literature*. New Delhi: Sterling.

Maso, Carole. "The Sylvia Lining." *Village Voice Literary Supplement*. Oct.-Nov. 2000.

Mckay, D.F. "Aspects of Energy in the Poetry of Dylan Thomas and Sylvia Plath." *The Critical Quarterly*. Vol. 16, no. 1. Spring 1974. 53-67.

Miller, Karl. "Ed in American Ego." *Times Literary Supplement*. Feb. 6, 1998. 7-9.

Oates, Jyoce Carol. "The Death Throes of Romanticism: The Poetry of Sylvia Plath." *Southern Review*. Vol. 9, no. 3. July 1973. Article revised on Nov. 16, 1999. Downloaded on 19.7.2001 from <www.usfca.edu/fac-staff/southerr/throes.html>

Plath, Sylvia. The *Bell Jar*. 1966. London: Faber and Faber. Hereafter cited as *BJ*.

______. *Letters Home*. 1976. Ed. Aurelia Plath. London: Faber and Faber. Hereafter cited as *LH*.

______. *Johnny Panic and the Bible of Dreams*. 1979. London: Faber and Faber. Hereafter cited as *JP*.

______. *Collected Poems*. 1981. Ed. Ted Hughes. London: Faber and Faber. Hereafter cited as *CP*.

______. *Journals*. 1983. Ed. Ted Hughes and Francis McCllough. New York: Ballantine Books. Hereafter cited as *J*.

Rich, Adrienne. 1976. *Of Woman Born: Motherhood as Experience and Institution*. New York: W.W. Norton.

Sagar, Keith. 2000. *The Laughter of the Foxes: A Study of Ted Hughes*. Liverpool: Liverpool Univ. Press.

Schneir, Miriam. Ed. 1995. *The Vintage Book of Feminism*. London: Vintage Books.

Steiner, Nancy. 1973. *A Closer Look at Ariel*. New York: Harper and Row.

Thwaite, Anthony. 1996. *Poetry Today: A Critical Guide to British Poetry 1960-1995*. London and New York: Longman.

"From a silence deep within": Kamala Das Surayya*

I must linger on
trapped in immortality
my only freedom being
the freedom to
discompose.

Kamala Das

On December 16, 1999 at the age of sixty-one, Kamala Das a high caste Nayar woman from the renowned Nalapat clan of Kerala, became a Muslim. A week later she was formally initiated into Islam by religious scholars from Malabar, at the Palayam mosque in Thiruvananthapuram and became Kamala Surayya, in a dramatic gesture that defied and shocked the Hindu orthodoxy. This maverick writer claims however, that conversion was not a sudden decision but arose out of a conviction. The idea, she says had been on her mind for twenty-seven years before she took the final plunge. The turning point had come during a visit to her friend Nusrat Jehan Begum's house in Mumbai, where she encountered a "strange fragrance" that pervaded the room of a sick, old member of the household. She recalls that it had fascinated her and had even inspired a story, "Atharinte Manam," which in Malayalam means 'Fragrance of Attar.'

"In my story and in my poems after that on the omniscient God, it is Islam that you will find. I even used to wear a veil on my tours abroad," says this bilingual writer, in an interview with

---

*A part of this paper has been taken from my earlier paper on the poet, "The Confessional Voice of Kamala Das" in *Perspectives on Kamala Das*, ed. Iqbal Kaur.

Charmy Harikrishnan. In exercising her choice the poet had quietly set "the cat among the pigeons," as Leela Menon puts it and invited in the bargain not only wide and wild publicity, both favorable and adverse, but also overt threats to her life. The poet has nevertheless remained unfazed and even wears the *burka* with elan now. A section of progressive Muslim women feel let down by her acceptance of the *purdah* and the usual somewhat regressive norms of the Muslim orthodoxy. Others, however, view her conversion as the crossing over of yet another frontier, more so in the face of stiff resistance against conversions from extremist Hindu groups. They see in the conversion of an upper-caste woman to a minority religion, evidence of commendable courage even though the act may seem tinged with eccentricity. For Surayya, however, the *burka* is as much a passport to anonymity as it is a "bullet-proof dress," an armor against "the piercing eyes of men." (Kaur 160) She confesses in an interview with Priya Pathiyan, that when she "wears the *burka* with the metal visor across [her] nose [she] can go anywhere be anyone. It gives [her] the anonymity [she] has always craved for." (*TOI*) This being able to go anywhere and be anyone, which translates into the chameleon poet's desire to explore varied sites associated with authentic female experience, becomes central to our understanding of Kamala Surayya's creative impulse. Her poetry seeks to lend voice to the aspirations, desires and plight of the millions of silent women who have not been able to find a voice. Whether her conversion was motivated by her decision to marry her young Muslim lover who decided instead to walk out on her, or by her "zest for a life with Allah" (Iype), is difficult to determine. What can be said with an element of certitude, however, is that she sees in it a rejuvenation of the spirit, a new birth and a new dream finding shape. She admits that she knew little about the religion when she adopted it but after studying the Koran she believes in its theology that "the truth must emerge" (Harikrishnan). She hopes that there will be a day when religious beliefs will not be held against anyone but will be a tribute to the person's moral strength.

The paradox of freedom in confinement then, is what best defines the life and literary career of Kamala Surayya, a poet who has always courted controversy. One of the first modernist writers to assert her femininity as a human in Indian literature, she has been something of a cult figure in her home state and a source of great inspiration and emulation for women with literary aspirations. For the poet, painter, activist and feminist (though she claims that she is "feminine" and not a feminist), among a lot of other things, life has been a long drawn battle against a religious and cultural orthodoxy that frowns upon the somewhat uninhibited life style of this apparently forthright person. Although her private life and her public stance cannot really be separated yet, also discernible in her writings are fictional images that derive from social reality. While she has always enjoyed voicing her pet hates and desires, the personal need not necessarily be her real self. She believes that the poet's raw material is neither stone nor clay but the poet's personality, yet the personal does not out-weigh the public concern of her art. "Whether something happened to me or to another woman is immaterial," she says. "What really matters is the experience, the incident. It may have happened to another woman who is probably too timid to write about it." (Kaur 168) As for her real self she has "no idea at all. It is as if I have been standing in front of a distorted mirror, one of those you find at fun-fares. So I have never seen the correct reflection of my face." (Kaur 168) Behind this seemingly innocuous comment, however, lies a statement of great import. Taking up the mirror as a metaphor of society Susan Stanford Friedman argues that "the mirror projects an image of WOMAN, a category which is supposed to define the individual woman's identity." (Qtd. Harish 26) That this category has been distorted further through patriarchal definitions, is quite evident from Surayya's lament in one of her earliest poems, 'Introduction':

Dress in sarees, be girl
Be wife, they said. Be embroiderer, be cook,
Be a quarreler with servants. Fit in. Oh,
Belong, cried the categorisers. (*CDN* 48)

Even though the publication of Surayya's autobiography *My Story* (1974), had evoked a host of extreme responses and earned her the notorious reputation of being a voyeur's delight, it would be unfair to dismiss a serious writer with such superficial readings. While her autobiography does to some extent encourage readers to identify the persona of the book unequivocally with the writer, it would be well to remember Nancy Chodorow's argument that women have no isolate selves. In *Psychoanalysis and the Sociology of Gender* (1978), she infers that men are trained to think "oppositionally," while women are taught to respond "relationally." She explores this bifurcation extensively in her book, contending that the concept of isolate selfhood is inapplicable to women who have fluid ego boundaries and form relational identities. This theory of collective selfhood finds support in the theories of Indian psychoanalysts like Sudhir Kakar, Indira Parikh and Ashish Nandy as well, in the context of identity formation in Indian women. In the light of this argument, *My Story* assumes greater significance than has been hitherto been accorded to it. The poet admits in an interview with Eunice de Souza that she will "not swear everything in that book happened to me," for she is a "practiced teller of white lies" (34). It would be useful then to read in the subtext of these confessions, the subliminal longings and desires as also the fate of every woman caught in the intricate web of power relationships with the concomitant pain, inadequacies, despair and frustrations therein. As Surayya writes in an early poem:

I have no joys which are not yours, no
Aches which are not yours. I too call myself I. (*EDS* 11)

More important for us to understand, then, is that what has been said is by and large the statement of a collective truth. In a personal letter dated October 30, 1985, the poet confesses that *My Story* had evoked "stony silences pregnant with wrath." It had disturbed her relatives and community to such an extent that her father had even threatened to commit suicide. "I come from a house of virtue," says the poet cynically. "My uncles, my brothers are all very 'good' people" (*TP* 37), so the book had cost "me many things that I held dear." (Preface to *My Story*) Nevertheless, she does not regret having written a word of it for "Malayali women do view themselves differently now. *My Story* has also contributed to this new emotional climate." (Kaur 159) Her autobiography thus stands as a watershed in post-Independence women's writing in India. With "uncompromising honesty [which] emerges as its most appealing force, especially when it is directed against herself," (Nabar 163) Surayya is willing to reveal the most intimate aspects of a woman's life. The book is a courageous act that marks a turning point, a new direction a new climate for more veracious, revelatory and confessional writings by women.

Sensationalism has always been part of Surayya's intent, need and strategy to jolt a complacent patriarchy and orthodoxy. Her life and writings have often aroused diverse and strong reactions that swing between the two extremes of admiration and outrage. Her fundamental rejection of the traditional Hindu woman's virtues, for a candid articulation of her sexuality and identity as a woman, has earned her the sobriquet of Kerala's 'Queen of Erotica.' Critics have written at length about her "desperate obsession with love," (Sarang 7) or "more appropriately with intimacy," which is "far removed from history, at a level where the larger realities of life yield place to the constricted world of the cloistered self." (Raveendran 81) This has made her "a prisoner of her own loneliness," says Dwivedi. (303) Some critics have been particularly concerned with her "promiscuous self-exposure," (Iyengar 713) her "frankness of manner in dealing with love and sex," (Sarang 27) and her "self-centered and unabashedly sexual" utterances. (Walsh 143) Others have focused on an "excess of emotion and self-dramatization" (King 156), and the "larger than life personality obsessive in its awareness of its self, yet creating a drama of selfhood." (King 147) Sunanda Chavan observes an "almost exclusive concern with the experience of personal love in her poetry." (*FV* 60) Vrinda Nabar reinforces the same idea when she states that in her later poetry Surayya "withdraws increasingly into a world of purely personal grievances. . . . because they are what her love poetry embodies" (163) and even shows an impatience with the poet's tiresome attitude and penchant for role-playing. While these observations are arguably true, it would be unfair to restrict the poet to a narrow confessionalism, while ignoring other significant dimensions that call for special consideration because of her unique place among the women poets of India. Surayya herself resents her slotting in the limited confines of sexual denominations and strongly disapproves of those who have stigmatized her as a sex symbol. "I have a number of social commitments, but everyone thinks only about sex in relation to my writing," she laments. (*TP* 33) "Pick up the phone and it is either a threatening call or one where a 27-year-old man professes his desire to meet me. They have all missed the point," she adds wryly (*TOI*). While love, sex and lust do form the thematic core of Kamala Surayya's writings these are not to be confused with obsessive libidinal urges and orientations. "Sex is a messy job," she declares (*TP*36), even while acknowledging its procreative function. Her creative urge extends far beyond "the sad lie of [her] unending lust" (*VS* 79), and other such simplistic interpretations. "I am not a physical person" she tells de Souza, adding candidly that she "never wrote about women's lust because [she] never felt it," but more important, because often women pretend, "in order to be part of the game" (*TP* 36). This whole dynamic she telescopes into a pithy statement in her poem, 'The Freaks':

> I am a freak. It's only
> To save my face, I flaunt, at
> Times, a grand, flamboyant lust. (*RP* 23)

In her conversation with de Souza she also confesses that although she did write about "men's lust" on her husband's insistence that she "Make it hot," she hated him for suggesting that she ought to write more for voyeuristic delight than with serious poetic intent.

In a devastating indictment of the poet, M. Prabha leads a strident group of detractors who have peremptorily dismissed Surayya's poetry, as the lewd outpourings of a woman smitten with her warped libidinal impulses. In a recently published book *The Waffle of the Toffs*, Prabha attributes the poet's success to both, a clever marketing of her "salacious commodity" ludicrously termed as "bedroom bardistry," that provides much desired entertainment to the "hungering Indian male" and to the right connections in the right places. "All her outpourings pertain to the pelvic region, which readily becomes a talking point in a cocktail circuit," states Prabha. The critic's censure is taken even further by imputing, that the poet's only claim to fame is the dubious distinction of being "the paparazzi's dream-girl" who has "pre-empted Shobha De in verse." (224-25) Such forceful invective coming from a writer who laments the dismal "famine" of "serious and informed criticism on Indian poetry in English," (224) does come as a surprise indeed. It is ironic that in one fell stroke Prabha has axed into a heap of dead wood, a courageous and significant poet who has learnt to ignore what people will think and say. "People think that the ideal woman is like a Hindi film heroine with a drought in her genitalia and over-moist eyes," says Surayya. "But real women are different. We are courageous." (*TOI*) Known for her frank and outspoken explorations of female sexuality, her poems, which have evoked genuine interest among serious readers are, often a rebellion against the sexual self-denial, which many cultures impose on their women. Perhaps it would do well at this juncture to illustrate through Germaine Greer's definition of the stereotypical woman, how women's sexuality has been pushed under the wraps by sexist and prudish identifications. In her book *The Female Eunuch*,

Greer argues that the fantasy stereotype created by men is nothing short of a castrated creature—a female eunuch. In her view she is "a sexual object . . . a doll. . . . [She] absolutely must be young, her body, her flesh buoyant and *she must not have a sexual organ.*" (Qtd. Schneir 344)

She states further that the process of her "desexualisation" involves not only her mind but her feelings also. In other words she must neither have intelligence nor have libido. Surayya's poetic agenda then, apparently lies in her aim and attempt to subvert such false representations of women and womanhood. Her very own dancing eunuchs are neither passive nor muted nor young. Beating their "sorry breasts," they sing melancholy songs in their harsh voices, of "Lovers dying and of children left unborn." They are not without sexual organs either, for:

> Beneath the fiery gulmohar, with
> braids flying, dark eyes flashing, they danced and
> They danced, oh, they danced till they bled. (*VS* 77-78)

It is quite evident that Surayya's detractors seem to have no special feel for the poet's work or worth and would rather conform to established identifications. Women's sexuality has often been shrouded in mystery and the poet's bold explorations in this direction have helped to strip the veil off the myth and the mystery. Contrary to the contention that her poetry "is a privy of her psyche," (Prabha 227) when Surayya makes an example of herself she is in fact speaking not for herself alone but for all of womankind. Any attempt to make a one-to-one equation with her life then would be to limit the scope and range of the poet through charlatan and superficial readings. And, Surayya herself declares unflinchingly that her poetry is for a targeted audience that is, "only for those who like to listen." What she narrates:

> are the ordinary
> events of an
> ordinary life. (*D* 33)

"The idea" she says, "is that we should write about myth and history." (*TP* 33) Her vast "sexual hungers," then are a poetic strategy for affecting an awareness of women's sexuality as it is and not as it has been made out to be. "For centuries women's sexuality has been masked and deformed by most observers, and never more so than in our time," says Greer. "The female is considered a sexual object for the use of other sexual beings, men. Her sexuality is both denied and misrepresented as passivity." (345) Greer presses her point further by suggesting that "Lovemaking has become a male skill, of which, women are the judges." (347) Poems like 'The Maggots' and 'The Descendants,' then become vantage locations for a satirical reconstruction of the supposedly pleasurable act of lovemaking:

> That night in her husband's arms Radha felt
> So dead that he asked, What is wrong,
> Do you mind my kisses love? and she said,
> No, not at all, but thought, What is
> It to the corpse if the maggots nip? (*D* 22)

Significantly, the choice of Radha as every woman is by design and no accident. In the sensuous and rebellious Radha determined to break social norms, albeit clandestinely, Indian women find an image they can readily internalize. Also, in her adulterous relationship with Krishna the object of every woman's fantasy, they find a particularly relevant structure that they can identify with. Likewise 'The Descendants,' too articulates the subconscious frustrations that are born out of repressed impulses and personalities:

> We have lain in every weather, nailed no not
> To crosses, but to soft beds against
> Softer forms, while the heaving, lurching,
> Tender hours passed in a half-dusk, half-dawn and
> Half-dream, half-real trance. We were the yielders
> Yielding ourselves to everything. (*EDS* 12)

No nymphomaniac however, the poet is neither suggesting nor trying to promote promiscuity, but just stating candidly that "sex does figure in the thoughts" (*TP* 34). As she writes in another poem:

> I'm not yours for the asking
> Grovel at my feet,
> remove your monkey-suits and dance,
> Sing Erato, Erato, Erato
> Yet I shall be indifferent. (*D* 31)

Nevertheless, with characteristic honesty, Surayya does not deny relationships for she admits that she "couldn't have written without them." (*TP* 36) She does however emphatically gainsay, that she entered into relationships to find writing material.

This brings to mind the most heavily stressed stereotype of 'deviant' femininity. An unconventional woman is invariably imaged by the dominant culture as a seductress, a woman who is sexually insatiable and deceitful in the service of her lust. It is this image that Surayya appropriates to reflect the dominant ideology, which reinforces stereotypical identifications, as well as to militate against it. She can thus state cynically in her poem 'Composition':

> With every interesting man I meet
> be it
> a curious editor,
> or a poet with a skin yellowed
> like antique paper,
> I must
> most deliberately
> Whip up a froth of desire
> a passion to suit the occasion.
> I must let my mind striptease
> I must extrude autobiography. (*D* 30)

Closely linked to the image of seductress is the image of woman as shrew—willful, scolding, domineering, angry. The poet argues that it is patriarchy that turns a woman into a shrew. One of the many suggestions she makes to thwart such falsified images of self-reliant women, is the return to a matriarchy in which women hold pivotal positions. Her wistful and fond remembrances of her matriarchal ancestry are thus linked directly, to her longing for a long lost tradition that she associates with a sense of order and innocence. She is painfully aware, however, of the futility of such desires that will remain elusive in a culture that validates only male experience. The memory of her dead grandmother, the "first" she loved, thus serves a dual purpose. It functions as a reminder of both, a dead tradition, as well as of the futility of all dreams associated with its revival. She discovers that her grandmother's:

> trunks, when opened, after
> she died, contained only dolls. (*D* 17)

Beneath an apparent brazenness then, lies the poet's serious and passionate desire to reinvent herself and in the process, other women as well. Tottering beneath the weight of a name "chosen by someone else," she rejects an imposed identity:

> Why should I remember or bear
> That sweet-sounding name pinned to
> Me, a medal, undeservingly
> Gained, at moments when, all of
> Me is ablaze with fire? (*CDN* 47)

This impulse to make anew is motivated and reinforced then, by a strong urge to put an end to the farce of passive, institutionalized womanhood:

> Woman, is this happiness, this lying buried
> Beneath this man? It' time to come alive
> The world extends a lot beyond his six-foot frame. (*D* 20)

Telling the truth about one's body is the most difficult of acts, more so in a reality where women pretend and lie even with their bodies, to keep their relationships. Surayya's poetic strength therefore, comes from a triumphant wrestling with patriarchal Identifications and as Harold Bloom would put it: "from an even greater solipsism" (Lodge 241). Thus, contrary to the contention that her "opuscules are bundles of narcissistic rant often bordering on hysteria" (Prabha 227), the poet's life and writings are a source of tremendous hope and strength for hundreds of women who have not been able to speak out, or about their experiences. With candor, she becomes their voice in a so-called civilized world in which female volition, desire and agency have literally been pushed into the margins. If her poetry has hitherto been viewed as a personal lament, it becomes imperative for us to see in it a reformist preoccupation as well, through the poet's imaginative identification with other women. The voice that speaks "From the silence somewhere deep within" (*CDN* 46), reminds us of the millions of voices that have been silenced for centuries:

> I am a million, million people
> Talking all at once, with voices
> Raised in clamour, like maids
> At village wells.
>
> I am a million, million deaths
> Pox-cluttered, each a dying seed
> Someday to be shed, to grow for
> Someone else, a memory.
>
> I am a million, million births
> Hushed with triumphant blood, each a growing
> Thing that thrusts its long-nailed hands
> To scar the hollow air.
>
> I am a million, million silences
> Strung like crystal beads
> Onto someone else's
> Song. (*CDN* 49)

The journey from her early 'Introduction' as "sinner" and "saint," "beloved" and "betrayed," to her incarnation as Kamala Surayya (the name means *saptarishi* or the Ursa Major, in Persian), has neither been easy nor free from disappointments. While it may not be possible to write with any measure of conclusiveness about a writer, it becomes even more difficult to put down the career and creative graph of a living and still-growing poet. A versatile woman who has experimented with various forms of art—poetry, fiction, drama, painting—she has now moved to being a newspaper columnist, a "professional writer," in order to "survive." With characteristic nonchalance she tells Shobha Warrier in a 1996 Rediff interview, that it is difficult to remain a poet because "poetry doesn't sell in this country." The poet's adoption of varied genres of expression has, however, contributed in large measure to her experience and imaginative enlargement. A shuffling, stumbling but still spirited 68-year-old Surayya debilitated with diabetic neuropathy and failing eyesight, is now busy birthing a new political party, Lok Seva, that will spread the message of love and truth. She believes that politics could be a possible conduit to the amelioration of hundreds of disadvantaged and distressed women.

Descending from the affluent matrilineal, matriarchal family of the Nalapat Nayars, Kamala Surayya was born on March 31, 1934, in Punnayurkulum, in South Malabar, in the state of Kerala. Her childhood memories revolve fondly around a "puritanical" grandmother who fed her on the myth of Krishna as her "greatest friend" (*TP* 36) and the Jnanapith Award-winner Balamani Amma, her suppliant, indifferent mother. She recalls that she came to be one of the most respected of Malayali women writers, a cult figure of sorts, for writing poems that "did not shock anyone." (*TP* 37) Among others, was also the not-so-pleasant memory of her domineering Gandhian father, *Mathrubhoomi* director V.M. Nair, who along with being snobbish about his children's education (Kaur 157), also forced her mother to wear khadi from the second day of their marriage. (*TP* 31) The poet talks candidly about the hypocritical relationship that her parents shared and their frequent nocturnal quarrels behind the facade of a happy marriage that consequently colored her childhood and adult life as well. Interestingly enough, despite belonging to a community in which, the matriarch is supposed to hold a central position, it was her father who called all the shots. Her community was as obsessed with the myth of male sovereignty as any patriarchal one. Fully aware of the privileges of a Nayar woman, the poet informs de Souza by way of illustration, that a Nayar woman could leave her husband's clogs outside the door if she no longer wanted him (37). Caught between the contrary pulls of an ideal matriarchy and an oppressive patriarchy in manner of practice, Surayya was rather disturbed by the fact that the matriarchs of her community lacked courage and had succumbed to unjust social pressures. Abdicating their advantaged status, they had accepted their subservient roles as well as their biology, as their destiny. Resultantly, she too was not brought up as a true Nayar woman. She regrets to date that her mother failed to give her the love, security and support she so desperately needed and even sided with her husband whenever there was a crisis (Kaur 161). The poet recalls bitterly that her father was autocratic and treated them like "menials" because he was the "family bread-winner." (*TP* 32) In the poet's recollection of her father, one can thus locate the surreptitious ways in which sexual colonialism operates through economic support and guardianship. The loss of the father is felt more materially than emotionally:

> We are tongue-tied, humbled and quiet
> Although within we wept for you
> And more for ourselves, now without a guardian. (*CP* 39)

Love too, which grows more out of gratitude for a provider than out of filial affection, is expressed as a somnambulistic refrain rather than as a deeply felt emotion:

> Who would send us money to bail us out of jail?
> Who would come when we land as junk at the
> city hospitals? (*CP* 39)

On the other hand, it is the memory of the grandmother, which evokes a profound sense of loss and emotional vacuum:

> There is a house now far away where once

I received love. . . . That woman died,
The house withdrew into silence.

. . . you cannot believe, darling
Can you, that I lived in such a house and
Was proud and loved . . . I who have lost
My way and beg now at stranger's doors to
Receive love at least in small change. (*CDN* 46)

Although the poet's sense of nostalgia in these poems is easily identifiable, yet in them is also discernible a decisive attempt to break free, to move on and refuse to remain mired in a tradition that lies trapped in a time warp:

My grandmother asked me to spend
one night in the old family home.
We shall talk, she said, darling
we shall talk all night.
She however adds without remorse:
My grandmother's lamp burned all night
on the window sill.
It is no use regretting now
or feeling ashamed. (*D* 32-33)

Educated privately, Surayya was married off at fifteen "as a punishment for not being able to do well in maths," (Kaur 161) to the much older Madhava Das, who was a consultant with the International Monetary Fund. Without being aware or even capable of comprehending the physical and emotional implications of her changed status, the poet deplores that she was thrown unceremoniously into the "murky waters" of matrimony (*TP* 36) and motherhood, which followed soon after:

I was a child and later they
Told me I grew
. . . When
I asked for love not knowing what else to ask
For, he drew a youth of sixteen into the
Bedroom and closed the door. He did not beat me
But my sad woman body felt so beaten. (*EDS* 10)

It was a loveless, companionless marriage, more like "dry toast," she tells de Souza wryly. Her husband left her free to choose her own company and occupy herself as best as she could. But strangely enough, she adds rather enigmatically, that it was a "good relationship." (*TP* 36) Surayya's often conflicting and paradoxical statements about her marriage and relationship with her husband underscore, not only the complex matrix of conjugal relationships, but also highlight the deep-rooted constraints that operate and inhibit expression no matter how sincere the attempt at honesty. Such prevarication is reflective of the powerful effects of acculturation and social prejudices that function imperceptibly, as powerful determinants of what may or may not be thought, revealed or even admitted as true. Her ambivalence coalesces, the prescriptive and the lived experience of matrimony even as it underpins the ambiguity of her social membership. Her initial inability is manifested in her failure to stall, or even protest against the scriptural prescription of marriage. The dubiety of child-marriage notwithstanding, marriage has never been an issue in the Indian cultural context and is also accepted as a sacred duty. Surayya's refusal later, to opt out of a relationship that had afforded her neither physical nor emotional and spiritual fulfillment, does however encourage serious deliberations on oppressive practices that continue unseen, unheard and what is even more alarming, unrecognized. Not surprisingly then, the poet justifies her option of staying on, as a form of empowerment through choice (160). Yet it raises a big question mark on the Hindu ethics of *shakti* (power) through suffering, which women are encouraged to believe in. The interconnectedness in the Hindu psyche, of empowerment and suffering and its validity as a religious structure through which, patriarchy sustains itself, encourages women to validate their own oppression by making a virtue of it. In actual manner of practice, this ethic is neither mutually inclusive nor extendable and exemplifies how religion mediates as an authoritative framework for women validating their own oppression. Also, it shows how womanhood is enmeshed in the production of national, religious and male identity, community and camaraderie. In this context it would be relevant to quote Niranjan Mohanty, who seems highly appreciative of the nature and "willing" subjugation of women in India. "There is something *miraculous,*" says Mohanty, in this "phenomenon of woman's subjugation to the family's male dominance. The Indian mother [read spouse as well] does not mind this subordination. *It instills in her an invisible strength, an unending patience and tolerance that overshadows the misdemeaning features of subordination* and makes her the key figure in bringing order, harmony, peace and prosperity to the family. Here lies the mystery of human relationships in the oriental context. One may legitimately feel that a *woman's subjugation is a willing phenomenon and it can negate any gender-ego.*" (48, my italics)

Such definitions that valorize the suffering and subjugation of women, are subtle forms of exploitation, which reinforce sexual hierarchies. Also, they are powerful channels through which Indian women are tokenized as figures of power, by allowing them to act out the fantasy of being in control, through the patriarchal pretence of male pliability. Thus, instead of trying to undo such deceptive identifications, women seek to reinforce them and all but unwittingly fall into the patriarchal trap of perpetrating their own subjugation. Resultantly, conflicts and dilemmas generated by the contrary responses of their real selves when suppressed either result in grave psychological problems, or get translated into more constructive forms of resistance. Surayya too, admits having made several unsuccessful attempts at suicide, but is also quick to add that pain and suffering has been the basis of her creativity. These experiences are effectively expressed in poems like 'Luminol' and 'Suicide.' For her, poetry thus becomes an effective medium for articulating the uneasy burden of perceived, partially perceived and unperceived configurations that go into the construction of a painful reality. Also, her medium reserves for her the right to peaceful resistance and possible revolution, by scratching epidermal relationships in a society of ritual pretense:

> I must pose
> I must pretend
> I must act the role
> Of happy woman,
> Happy wife. (*D* 2)

Her resentment against institutionalized marriage and its enforced cohabitation, comes across sharply in a poem like 'Of Calcutta' in which, she questions the very foundations of such unwilling alliances:

> I was sent away to protect a family's
> Honour, to save a few cowards, to defend some
> Abstractions, sent to another city to be
> A relative's wife, a hausfrau from his home and
> A mother for his sons, yet another nodding
> Doll for his parlour, a walkie talkie one to
> warm his bed at night.

In yet another poem 'The Doubt,' her anger at the unequal terms of such relationships spills forth unambiguously, even while it raises the perturbing but vital question of marital rape:

> And what am I in sex who shuttles
> Obsessively from his
> Stabs to recovery
> In her small silent room? (*D* 16)

Kamala Surayya's poem, 'The Looking Glass,' which has been anthologized frequently as an illustration of a sexual candor "unusual in the Indian context," (Parthasarathy 22) holds the key to an in depth understanding of her poetic impulse and purpose. The poem, which is a scathing comment on the destructive powers of patriarchy, addresses the complex problem of self-representation and the adverse effects of an acculturation that denies women a perception of their real selves. The looking glass is one of the poet's most searing symbols and is imbued with several layers of meaning. It becomes an ambivalent metaphor for the real and the distorted image of the woman that it reflects back. While it is an instrument for the reassurance and validation of man's isolate self, for the woman it is a surface prescribing a stereotyped role, for it throws back an image that represents a well defined category rather than an individual:

> Gift him what makes you woman, the scent of
> Long hair, the musk of sweat
> between the breasts,
> The warm shock of menstrual blood, and all your
> *Endless female hungers.* (*RP* 27, my italics)

The poet inaugurates the poem significantly, with the ancient 'scientific,' *Kamasutric* prescription of how to 'seduce' and keep your *only* man:

> Getting a man to love you is easy
> Only be honest about your wants as
> *Woman.* Stand nude before the glass *with him*
> So that *he sees himself the stronger one*
> *And believes it so,* and you so much
> Softer, younger, lovelier. . . . *Admit*
> *Your Admiration.* (*RP* 27, my italics)

The weight of this 'time-honored' wisdom however, rests precariously on the passive admission, admiration and submission of the woman, even while it reinforces the ambiguous ethics of *shakti* through suffering by setting up an ironic contrast between male virility and female malleability. On the level of statement, the poem is a lyrical expression of sexual love. Nevertheless, on the sub textual level, it explodes several myths. The sardonic tone itself, functions as a poetic strategy that transforms a surface lyricism into a stark comment on media-evoked, romanticized versions of gender relations and alerts the reader to underlying patriarchal assumptions. The tenor of the poem, thus, sets into motion the whole process of abrogation and appropriation. By applying well-established canons of womanhood, the poet underscores the unequal terms of gender relationships. Please your man is the poet's professed message, but remember your power to please him, is the underlying and empowering purpose. This very message she conveys overtly in a poem like, 'The Stone Age':

> And
> Yet on daydreams, strong men cast their shadows,
> they sink
> Like white suns in the swell of my Dravidian blood. (*EDS 16*)

Through the subversive manoeuvers of dissimulation, mimicry, parody and self-effacing diminution, the poet exposes the subtle ways in which patriarchy validates and sustains itself. By deliberately setting up dualities, the poet is not only interrogating patriarchal surmises but also investigating the postulates by which these codes are imposed and maintained. The concluding lines of 'The Looking Glass' are, thus, a poignant reminder and denunciation of a scriptural tradition 'written by men' whereby a widow, a woman without *her* man that is, is condemned to a "drab," colorless and "destitute" existence of enforced celibacy aimed at containing her sexuality:

> Oh yes, getting
> A man to love is easy, but living
> Without him afterwards may have to be
> Faced. . . .
> your
> Body which once under his touch had gleamed
> Like burnished brass now drab and destitute. (*RP* 27)

Like most of the other poems then, 'The Looking Glass' too is not dyed in the flaming colors of erotica, in which the poet struts around wearing her morals on her sleeve, but is a serious poem with a much deeper intent. The poem affects an exposé of sexual relations from a woman-centered point of view. The overt and calculated emphasis on intimate physical details including the supposedly 'sex-appeal-oozing' ablutionary ones too, functions as a reminder of significant absences, that is the invisible text of principles not drawn from patriarchy's rule book, rather than as amatory gesture. By prizing open social complexities that are shrouded, the poem offers a sad but caustic commentary on sanitized, universalistic histories in which women have been controlled and programmed to accept a pre-determined fate.

Kamala Surayya's fascination to her readers also lies in her uncanny explorations of love, which alters within varying contexts, in the multifaceted mosaic of life. She claims to have launched her love poetry quite early in life, with a poem she wrote to her forty-eight-year-old English teacher while still in school. When her first volume of poems *Summer in Calcutta* (1965) appeared, reviewers and readers alike found it unsettling. This was on account of the volume's marked shift of emphasis in form and sensibility, from that of earlier poets and its transparent sexual overtones, which they feared, would wield adverse influence on other women. The poet, however, was unapologetic about breaking free from the defined forms and modes of the first generation figures. She declares quite candidly in an interview, that love is "the only ritual I believe in, it makes everything legitimate." (*TOI*) In another interview she states with even greater conviction that love "creates its own climate." (Kaur 163) With rare frankness the poet expresses her views on the regenerative powers of love, which takes on the form of a search for an ideal union leading to the sublimation of carnal love. Whether she speaks as a wife or beloved, her poems, as Eunice de Souza rightly observes, have a "brooding intensity which has seldom been matched." (*TP* 40) This poetic strength is traceable as much to unrequited love as it is to a passionate desire for "a kind of love that is pervasive—all pervasive like ether." (Kaur 163). The search for an ideal union, in which sexual difference ceases to control, however, remains an elusive, ever-receding dream that invariably ends in the blind alley of gender-divided relations. Sadly enough, the poet believes that in all heterosexual relationships "each/rage(s) to burn the other out." (*D* 20) It is:

> Always the same, he serves his love in lethal doses

For love is Narcissus at the water's edge, haunted
By its own lonely face, and yet it must seek at last
And end, a pure, total freedom, it must will the mirrors
To shatter. (*EDS* 16)

Her love poems take the reader through a roller coaster journey of passionate, lusty interludes with their attendant betrayals that always end in failure to achieve spiritual communion. The poetic persona moves compulsively but in vain, from one substitute to another:

not to gather knowledge
Of yet another man . . . but to learn
What I was
Nevertheless:
. . . every
Lesson you gave me was about yourself. . . . .
Beneath your monstrous ego I ate the magic loaf
and
Became a dwarf. I lost my will and reason. (*EDS* 15-16)

The added weight of a spectral half existence with the other, hence compounds the already heavy burden of infidelity. Love lures irresistibly, but fails to satisfy. It becomes a "swivel-door" rejecting one lover, admitting another until:

I lost count, for always in my arms
Was a substitute for a substitute. (*D* 7)

The "substitute," which runs like a leitmotif in these poems is then, quintessentially reflective of the "Soul's lonely hunger." Love invariably degenerates into lust, which consumes to a point of disease. Her nocturnal encounters hold no promise of lasting love. She is even denied the comfort of a sustaining friendship. This failure to establish a mythical link with the other is expressed therefore, as a desperate desire to be subsumed by the "vortex of the sea" where "only the soul knows how to sing." The poet even contemplates suicide as the only release from this life of spiritual emptiness:

The sea's hostile cold
Is after-all skin-deep.
The sea's inner chambers
are all very warm.
There must be a sun slumbering
At the vortex of the sea. (*D* 2)

Love performs another function apart from the usual erotic and intimate one. It fills a void in the absence of God. It represents a human agency capable of restoring form and grace to the lover but remains nevertheless, elusive and almost impalpable. This search for an unrealizable ideal, then, informs her love poetry with a restless and agonized eroticism, remembered and evoked. The overall concern is the dreadful inability of love to prevail under the dominating concreteness of everyday life. The poem 'Words,' effectively presents this contrast in terms of the insubstantiality of words and the concreteness of objects and bodies:

All round me are words, and words and words,
They grow on me like leaves, they never
Seem to stop their slow growing
From within. . . . But I tell myself, words
Are a nuisance, beware of them, they
Can be so many things. (*CDN* 46)

In this context then, Surayya's Krishna poems too assume greater significance as embodying not a desperate plea for sexual communion, but for Krishna's ethics of self-reliance or *swadharma* (own norm, own morality), a key concept in the *Bhagvad Gita.* The poet has realized that just as the notion of ideal love is a myth, so also could the notion of Krishna as an "idealized phallus," (Kakar 144) just "be a myth." (*TP* 37) Desire and passion, however intense, cannot be sustained forever in the plurality of evolutionary mutations in which each phase has its own dominant pursuits and emotions. A mellower Surayya acknowledges now, that sex goes through the natural rhythms of the year in man and woman, ceaselessly changing. She has learnt that "love comes in different forms . . . spreading out, touching many people" (*TOI*). Krishna then, becomes a manifestation of this love:

> You have led me along a route
> I have never known before
> But at each turn when I near you
> Like a spectral flame you vanish. (*CP* 93)

It is this expansive, all-encompassing love, which enables her to say in a poem like 'Composition':

> I have reached the age in which
> one forgives all.
> I am ready to forgive friends
> their loving
> forgive those who ruined friendships. (*D* 33)

The kaleidoscopic images of women in Surayya's poetry account for its realism. She presents woman in her many roles as wife, beloved, mother, streetwalker, goddess—lovelorn, ecstatic, despondent, hoping, despairing, whoring, enduring—caught up in the vortex of her passions. The impulse is to remain authentic to the truth as she sees it. While many would dispute that Surayya's life is an embodiment of the state of women in India or elsewhere, there is little doubt that her speculations on the love-hate relationships that she shares with men, are brought to a climax in the central insight of her poetry:

> We are all alike,
> We women
> in our wrappings of hairless skin. (*D* 32)

This generalization, which transcends private fact, lifts her poetry into the realm of universal truth. Her concern with the wider universe of women transforms the personal voice into a grandiose impersonality that rescues it from degenerating into a fuddled, private lament. What the poet seems to imply is that those wonderful, thoughtful women who make such good companions to men are, after all, only sitting on the craters of their own volcanoes. The subtle imposition of a cultural framework enables a peep into the roaring fires within. Free from both, oriental mysticism and callow hysterics, her poetry gives a remarkable account of her innermost desires and frustrations. She herself is priest and confessor, saint and sinner, beloved and betrayed. If the substitute is every man in his lust, the victim is every "old wife turned whorish" (*D* 18), struggling to withdraw from under him. An artistic alchemist who was able to blend creativity and controversy, Kamala Surayya remains one of the sanest mega-celebrities among Indian writers.

Works Cited

Abraham, Abu. "Kamala Suraiya." *The Tribune.* January 2, 2000.

Bloom, Harold. "Poetic Origins and Final Phases." *Modern Criticism and Theory: A Reader.* David Lodge, ed. 1992. New York: Longman. 241-52.

Chavan, Sunanda P. 1984. *The Fair Voice: A Study of Indian Women Poets in English.* New Delhi: Sterling.

______. "Modern Indian English Women Poets: An Overview" *Perspectives on Indian Poetry in English.* M.K. Naik, ed. 1990. New Delhi: Abhinav. 190-207.

Chodorow, Nancy. 1978. *The Reproduction of Mothering: Psychoanalysis and the Sociology of Gender.* Berkley: The University of California Press.

Das, Kamala. 1975. *My Story.* New Delhi: Sterling.

______. 1965. *The Descendants.* Calcutta: Writers' Workshop. Hereafter cited as *D.*

______. 1984. *Collected Poems.* Trivandrum: Navkerala. Hereafter cited as *CP.*

de Souza, Eunice. Ed. 1997. *Nine Indian Women Poets: An Anthology.* New Delhi: Oxford University Press. Hereafter cited as *EDS.*

______. 1999. *Talking Poems: Conversations with Poets.* New Delhi: OUP. Hereafter cited as *TP.*

Dwivedi, A.N. 1978. *Indo-Anglian Poetry.* Allahabad: Kitab Mahal.

Greer, Germaine. 1970. *The Female Eunuch.* New York: McGraw-Hill.

Harikrishnan, Charmy. "High Priestess of Love" *The Week.* December 26, 1999.

Harish, Ranjana. "In the Cultural Hall of Mirrors: Issue of Gender, Genre Incompatibility in Women's Autobiography." *The Literary Criterion*. Vol. XXXI, no. 182. 1996. 25-32.

Iype, George. "When the temptress dawns the *purdah.*" December 14, 1999. Rediff on the Net.

Iyengar, K.R.S. 1999. *Indian Writing in English.* New Delhi: Sterling.

Jain, Jasbir. Ed. 1999. *Women's Writing: Text and Context.* Jaipur: Rawat.

Kakar, Sudhir. 1989. *Intimate Relations: Exploring Indian Sexuality.* New Delhi: Viking.

Kaur, Iqbal. Ed. 1995. *Perspectives on Kamala Das's Poetry.* New Delhi: Intellectual.

King, Bruce. 1994. *Modern Indian Poetry in English.* New Delhi: OUP.

Lodge, David. Ed. 1992. *Modern Criticism and Theory: A Reader.* New York: Longman.

Menon, Leela. "The Freedom and Bondage of Madhavikkutty." *The Indian Express*. December 19, 1999. Hereafter cited as *IE.*

Mohanty, Niranjan. "A Feminist Perspective on Kamala Das's Poetry." *Perspectives on Kamala Das's Poetry.* 45-66.

Nabar, Vrinda. 1994. *The Endless Female Hungers.* New Delhi: Sterling. Hereafter cited as *EFH.*

__________. "A View of Kamala Das." *Perspectives on Indian Poetry in English.* 158-68.

Naik, M.K. 1984. *Dimensions of Indian English Literature.* New Delhi: Sterling. Hereafter cited as *DIEL.*

__________. Ed. 1984. *Perspectives on Indian Poetry in English.* New Delhi: Abhinav. Hereafter cited as *PIPE.*

Narasimhaiah, C.D. Ed.1990. *An Anthology of Commonwealth Poetry.* Madras: Macmillan India. Hereafter cited as *CDN.*

Parthasarathy, R. Ed. 2000. *Ten Twentieth Century Poets.* New Delhi: OUP. Hereafter cited as *RP.*

Pathiyan, Priya. "Interview with Kamala Das." *The Times of India Sunday Review.* April 1, 2001. Hereafter cited as *TOI.*

Prabha, M. 2000. *The Waffle of the Toffs: A Sociocultural Critique of Indian Writing in English.* New Delhi: Oxford and IBH.

Rajan, P.K. Ed. 1995. *Changing Traditions in Indian English Literature.* New Delhi: Creative.

Raveendran, P.P. "Kamala Das: The Ideology of Intimacy." *Changing Traditions in Indian English Literature.* 81-91.

Sarang, V. Ed. 1995. *Indian English Poetry since 1950: An Anthology.* Bombay: Orient Longman. Hereafter cited as *VS.*

Schneir, Miriam. Ed. 1995. *The Vintage Book of Feminism.* London: Vintage.

Singh, Mina Surjit. "The Confessional Voice of Kamala Das." *Perspectives on Kamala Das's Poetry.* 89-98.

Walsh, William. 1990. *Indian Literature in English.* London and New York: Longman.

Warrier, Shobha. "Interview with Kamala Das." 1996. Rediff on the Net.

The Poetics of Democracy: Adrienne Rich*

In my sixty-fifth year I know something about language
it can eat or be eaten by experience
Medbh, poetry means refusing
the choice to kill or die
but the life of continuing is for the sane mad
and the bravest monsters.

Adrienne Rich

To do justice to the creative graph of as formidable an artist as Adrienne Rich within the confines of a short essay as this is a daunting task indeed. Yet, no study of American women's poetry would be complete without including the work of this major poet, theorist, early feminist, outspoken lesbian and political writer. Rich received the Lifetime Achievement Award from the Lannan Foundation in 1991 and has served as a role model for a whole generation of poets and activists. This essay attempts, what can best be defined as a thumb nail account of the poet's literary and social concerns as reflected in the vast corpus of her writings. In an essay entitled "Credo of a Passionate Skeptic," in the *Los Angeles Times* dated March 11, 2001, the poet has made a significant observation about our times which might just as well define the scale, sweep and ramifications of the poet's own art. Referring to Karl Marx as "a great geographer of the human condition," Rich states that Marx's depiction of the dehumanizing effects of early nineteenth century capitalism on the social landscape rings "truer than ever at the century's end." She says that for "Westerns to look back on 1900 is to come full face

---

*A part of this paper has been taken from my earlier paper entitled "The Poetry of Adrienne Rich" published in *The Aligarh Journal of English Studies* Vol. 19 no.1 1997.

upon ourselves in 2000." In a poetic career spanning more than fifty years, Rich's poetry too, comes to rest like a homing pigeon where it began, that is, in its major engagement with "trying to change the laws of history," as she states in an early autobiographical poem, 'Sources.'

Rich started out as a feminist but soon declared that her "thinking was unable to fulfill itself with feminism alone" (*LA Times*). Feminism was a natural extension of her poetry. She had realized that there could be no single-issue campaigns when there was a pressing need for writers and activists to be constantly conscious of being part of a larger network in a fast-shrinking global reality. She had begun to see the women's movement as a much more multicultural movement. Besides, she did not wish to be labeled for "labels get kind of lodged in a certain point of time and appear to contain only a certain content, and they lose their fluidity, they lose their openness and then the new generation comes along and wants to register its own experience in its own way." (Rothschild 5)

Rich therefore moved on to a much wider canvass, offering an elaborate defense of the fusion between poetry and politics, which coincided with her personal and poetic evolution and the tremendous force of the historical moment. The women's movement, Rich tells Paulo da Costa in a recent interview in the *Samsara Quarterly*: "appeared at a very crucial moment of my life. There was a whole political movement asking such questions. . . . I began to feel heard in that movement . . . because my voice was resonating with other voices." Poetry thus came to be seen as "a theatre of voices, not . . . coming from a single 'I' or from any one position" (8). Although the focus of her later works shifts to the system of social and demographic power relations, her critique of establishment norms and commitment to radical politics is, after all, homologous with the feminist critique of patriarchal power and policies. Like other radical movements by repressed groups, second wave feminism too was engaged in unscrolling a map on which race, class and gender intersected. In

Rich's mind, the women's movement was analogous with an imaginative identification with all women, with empathy, with the Keatsian quality of "negative capability" or what she terms as the "weak ego boundaries" (*ARP* 115), from which spring the most profound revolutions. Her earlier work thus provides the background against which her later work is fore-grounded and indicates certain directions in the poet's thinking aimed at rupturing the "dominant culture by focusing on the signifier and not the signified" as Rachael Blau Du Plessis would put it (7). Rich views herself as an artist with an "oppositional imagination" and a voice that does not speak the official language. Essentially anti-patriarchal, she believes that art is a self-transforming and regenerative process. It is a form of activism for social justice, given the extreme polarization of our social and imaginative life, that is, the community in which all art is rooted imitatively or oppositionally. Her argument is not with herself alone, for she believes in the inseparability of art from acute social crisis. Preferring to use the term 'women's liberation' to 'feminism,' she sees the movement "as potentially the ultimate democratizing force [that] involves justice on so many levels because of the way women interpenetrate everywhere" (Rothschild 6). Feminism is the remedial therapy for the distortions of patriarchal ideologies, which she attributes to male subjectivity. Men are "neither objective, nor value free, nor inclusively 'human'" (*LSS* 207). She still believes in what she wrote thirty years back in her essay "When We Dead Awaken: Writing as Re-Vision," in which she emphasized the need for "a change in the concept of sexual identity" if we are not to see "the old patriarchal order re-assert itself in every revolution." Our need to know the literature of the past is "not to pass on a tradition but to break its hold over us" (*ARP* 90-91) she reiterates.

Having witnessed the violence, exploitation and injustice of our difficult times, issues that have been burgeoning at specific times in history, have engaged Rich with the passionate commitment and conviction of one who has tried to live and render her times conscientiously, in the language of art. As she writes in a 1970 poem 'A Valediction Forbidding Mourning':

> When I think of a landscape I am thinking of a time.
> When I talk of taking a trip I mean forever. (*ARP* 54)

While her poetry charts the course of her passage from the "unconscious into the sayable, into the actable" (Martin *AAT* 169), her prose outlines a conscious understanding of that process. What makes this prolific writer tick is a genuine concern for all those who wish to claim wider horizons and participate in building a more inclusive and hopeful social order. The Civil Rights Movement, the protest against the Indo-China war, the Bay of Pigs incident, the Vietnam War, the Sit-ins and marches in the South, had all affected Rich profoundly. More importantly, the emergent women's movement and the gay/lesbian movement along with these political and social movements gathering force throughout the Sixties, all educated her in "the possibilities of an engaged art" (Prince). Rich's feelings of personal conflict, sexual alienation and cultural oppression, thus began to find increasing articulation in the larger context of her social and political reality. While the violence against the Black struggle for justice and dignity brought upon an awareness of how "racism deforms the racist," it also gave shape to a spirit of active participation in social change. It is this "participatory spirit, critical and activist," that Rich links to artistic creation (Prince). The Eighties were dominated by the same visibly shrinking democratic process through the economic policies of Ronald Reagan, which had opened the way to out-of-control corporate power. "Reaganomics," as Rich cynically terms these policies, had encouraged an exclusive rather than a more inclusive spirit of participation, with access to resources vested in fewer and fewer hands as a result of which the divide between the rich and poor had become more pronounced than ever before. Rich thus believes that the lived effects of an economic system "out of control and anti-human to the core," show how the history of the United States has been "a double history of selective and unequal arrangements." (*The Nation*) In this great flow of capitalism, the last decade of the twentieth century, which began with the Gulf war, has witnessed large-scale violence, a growing and predatory consumerism and an accelerated social disintegration. This has stunned right-minded people, writers and activists alike and at a time when Marxism seems to have lost its relevance, Rich finds his words very much alive. She had discovered a fusion of Marx's humanism with contemporary feminism, in her reading of Raya Dunayevskaya's vivid and incisive account of the "concrete revolutionary lives of women," and this she says "expanded [her] sense of the possibilities of both" (*LA Times* 4). Although Rich claims that she found no "blueprint for a future utopia" in Marxian ideology, yet it did provide a "skilled diagnosis of skewed and disfigured human relationship" (*LA Times* 3). This rapid coming apart during the years of the Nineties is captured trenchantly in a poem, 'The Shattered Head' from her 1999 volume, *Midnight Salvage*:

> Shattered head on the breast
> of a wooden hill
> Laid down there endlessly so
> tendrils soaked into mattered compose
> became a root.
> torqued over the faint springhead
> groin whence illegible
> matter leaches: worm-borings, spurts
> of silt
> volumes of sporic changes
> hair long blown into far follicles
> blasted into a chosen place
>
> Revenge on the head . . .
> revenge on the mouth . . .
> revenge on the eyes . . .
> revenge on the big searching lips
> the tender tongue
> revenge on the sensual, on the nose
> the

carrier of history
revenge on the life devoured
in another incinerator.

The poem is a lyric that calls up the season and gives a harrowing account of the condition of the world, not just America or Europe. It is therefore a desperate appeal to reason, to sanity and to "a desire for common welfare and public happiness above the balance sheet of profit." (*The Nation* 2) Her despair and anger at American culture coexists with her wish for a renewed vision of American commonality. This public happiness, which Rich terms elsewhere as "radical happiness," is perceived as any event that "inspires people all over the country." It is the "happiness of true participation in society, which would be possible for everyone" she tells Michael Klein in her June 1999 interview published in the *Boston Phoenix*. In the process of change, the public would also constitute ordinary men and women, those torn between bitterness and hope, who are reading poetry because they need it.

Among other things, Rich's sincerity of intent manifests in the stand she has often taken against the establishment. Most recent in a long history of dissension was her refusal in 1997, to accept the National Medal for the Arts awarded by the President of the United States, Bill Clinton. The refusal came as a mark of protest against the failure of the leadership at White House to live up to the true spirit of democracy. Explaining her position in an essay entitled "Why I refused the National Medal for the Arts," a month after being offered the Award, she wrote:

> My "no" came directly out of my work as a poet and essayist and citizen drawn to the interfold of personal and public experience. I had recently been thinking about the growing fragmentation of the social compact, of whatever this country had ever meant when it called itself a democracy. . . . There is no political leadership in the White House or the Congress that has spoken to and for the people who, in a very real sense, have felt abandoned by their government. (*LA Times BS*)

In her letter to Jane Alexander, then head of the National Endowment for the Arts too, she had declined the coveted award stating politely but categorically, that she could not accept such an award because:

> The very meaning of art as I understand it, is incompatible with the cynical politics of this administration. . . . Anyone familiar with my work from the early Sixties on knows that I believe in art's social presence—as a breaker of official silences, a voice for those whose voices are disregarded, and as a human right. . . . the art of poetry means nothing if it simply decorates the dinner tables of power which holds it hostage. . . . A President cannot meaningfully honor certain token artists while the people at large are so dishonored. . . . I don't think we can separate art from overall human dignity and hope. My concern for my country is inextricable from my concern as an artist. I could not participate in a ritual, which would feel so hypocritical to me. (*NY Times*).

Born in Baltimore, Maryland on May 16, 1939, Rich now shares her modest home on the outskirts of Santa Cruz, California, with the Caribbean-born teacher and novelist Michelle Cliff. In more than half a century of writing and almost twenty volumes of verse, Rich has come a long way from the post-war formalism of her first volume, *A Change of World* (1951). In his preface to the volume, which W.H. Auden had selected for inclusion in the Yale Younger Poet Series, he had praised Rich's "versification" and her "intuitive grasp of much subtler and more difficult matters like proportion, consistency of diction and tone." He had stated further that the poems were: "neatly and modestly dressed, speak quietly but do not mumble, respect their elders, but are not cowed by them and do not tell fibs" (*CW* 11). The poems in this volume illustrate the unconscious tensions and conflicts that Rich experienced as a young poet and formalism at that time was a strategy she adopted for handling themes she couldn't dare to touch otherwise. The conscious craft of these poems was, thus, a device to keep intense feelings at bay. She had also refrained from excessive sentimentality and from making a personal statement, for she had then believed that a poet must exercise emotional restraint. However, she was soon to discard this early formalism in favor of a more personal idiom, which enabled her to identify with and reach out to millions of women who shared her plight, investing thereby, a new confidence in the personal as political. Through the cultural deconstruction of *The Will to Change* (1971) and *Diving into the Wreck* (1973), and the lesbian-feminist reconstruction in *The Dream of a Common Language* (1978) and *Your Native Land, Your Life* (1986), her poetry has evolved today into a passionately political force for moral good. Her latest volumes—*An Atlas of the Difficult World* (1991), *Dark Fields of the Republic* (1995), *Midnight Salvage* (1999) and *Fox: Poems 1998-2000* (2001), all explore the possibility of poetry to "persist as a ligatory art rather than as an echo chamber of fragmentation and alienation" (*LA Times*). Her poetic concerns, then, begin with the personal as political but gradually grow into a radical commitment to social and political concerns, without sacrificing either the complexity of subjective experience or the intensity of personal emotion. Rich now sees the role of the poet as compatible with the role of the revolutionary because she understands, as Erica Jong suggests, that the "most profound revolutions will come from the development of our capacity for empathy" (172).

Adrienne Rich had written her most declarative feminist essay "When We Dead Awaken" in 1979, when as an eminent feminist she was invited by The Commission on the Status of Women to talk on "The Woman Writer in the Twentieth Century." She had borrowed the title of her essay from Henrik Ibsen's last and most controversial play, *When We Dead Awaken.* Rich had observed that the play was "about the use the male artist and thinker—in the process of creating culture as we know it—has made of women in his life and in his work." It was also about "a woman's slow struggling awakening to the use to which her life has been put." (*ARP* 90) She argued that for women to be recognized as artists in their own right, a change in the concept of sexual identity and a redefining of the parameters of love was essential. "Where woman has been a luxury for man, and has served as the painter's model, the poet's muse, but also as comforter, nurse, cook, bearer of his seed, secretarial assistant and copyist of his manuscripts, man has played quite a different role for the female artist" (*ARP* 92), she said. This whole process of change in outlook, of seeing afresh, of re-vision, of looking back into the "elemental humus of memory, dreams, art where there are no bygone eras" (*LA Times*) then, becomes crucial to our understanding of the poet's creative process. The battle against a divisive patriarchy she believes, can only be won by re-writing patriarchal myths, for writing is renaming, re-visioning. This process, which she defines as "the act of looking back, of seeing with fresh eyes, of entering an old text from a new critical direction," in her view, is "more for us than a chapter in cultural history: it is an act of survival. Until we understand the assumptions in which we are drenched we cannot know ourselves" (*ARP* 90). This looking back thus entails an exploration of the battered hulk of sexual definitions and obsolete myths, that is:

> the wreck and not the story of the wreck
> The thing itself and not the myth (*ARP* 67)

The instrument of that exploration would very naturally be the poet then:

> trying to translate pulsations
> into images for the relief of the body
> and reconstruction of the mind (*ARP* 46)

The year Rich wrote this essay significantly was also the year in which she walked out of a seemingly happy marriage. Although she cared a great deal about her husband and children, the dichotomy between fulfilling traditional female roles and the subversive function of the imagination was particularly painful as she sought ways in which the "energy of creation and the energy of relation [could] be united." (*ARP* 96) When she walked out on her husband the renowned Harvard economist Alfred Conrad, he had committed suicide, later the same year. Conrad had not opposed Rich's poetry writing, but it was quite clearly not as important as his own career. Rich recollects bitterly that her husband was an affectionate and sensitive man, who:

> unusual in the professional, academic world of the Fifties—was willing to "help." But it was clearly understood that his "help" was an act of generosity, that *his* work, *his* professional life, was the real work in the family. . . . I understood that my struggles as a writer were a kind of luxury, a *peculiarity of mind.* (*OWB* 27)

The consequent pain and anger of a creative, thinking woman in a culture that had denied her the most essential aspects of her experience, therefore helped Rich tremendously, to evolve as a person and an artist. This process of evolution, as Wendy Martin rightly suggests, involved her passage through "self-analysis, individual assertion and accomplishment, to rejection of patriarchal values, feminist activism and finally to building a woman-centered community." (*ATT* 168)

When *Snapshots of a Daughter-in-Law* was published in 1963 and won her the Hokin Prize for poetry, it earned negative response from critics who said the book was too personal, too bitter. Rich reiterates, however, that she "knew this was material that would have to find a place in [her] poetry, in [her] work, that it was probably central to it—as it indeed came to be." (Rothschild 4) In the poems of this volume, she was for the first time able to write directly about experiencing herself as a woman. *Snapshots* was a compelling and epiphanic work, which forced her to recognize women's marginalisation. It attempted to trace the relationship between gender and social values and economic reality, an analysis she continued to pursue through *Necessities of Life, Poems,* and *Leaflets,* as well. Resultantly the volumes changed her whole mode of writing from the forced rhythms and terse material forms of her earlier verse, to fragmentary compositions written in fierce snatches during the time available between household chores. Rich considers the title poem of the volume as her "first overtly feminist poem" (Rothschild 4).

When she put that poem down on paper, all the compounded rage of questions of identity, sacrifice, ego, creation, ambition was expended. It was "an extraordinary relief to write that poem," she says, even though it was "too literary, too dependent on allusion," for it was written at a time when she "hadn't found the courage yet to do without authorities." (*ARP* 97) *Snapshots*, which was eight years in writing, began to scrutinize women's position and its psychic, emotional and political consequences, as well as women's relationships to one another and stands as a watershed in Rich's poetic development:

> Well she's long about coming who must be
> more merciless to herself than history,
> Her mind full to the wind I see her plunge
> breasted and glancing through the currents,
> taking the light upon her
> at least as beautiful as any boy
> or helicopter,
> poised, still coming,
> her fine blades making the air wince. (*ARP* 16-17)

For the first time in this volume, in a more free and intimate language, Rich "situates her materials and emotions against the themes of language, boundaries, resistance, escape, and moments of life-altering choice" (Pope). As she contends in her poem, 'Prospective Immigrants Please Note':

> Either you will
> go through this door
> or you will not go through
>
> If you go through
> there is always the risk
> the risk of remembering your name. . . .
> but much will blind you,
> much will evade you,
> at what costs who knows?
>
> The door itself
> makes no promises.

It is only a door. (*ARP* 21)

Snapshots, thus, anticipated the intense struggle for personal integrity and political understanding that characterizes her work now. Stylistically too, the volume marked a transition from the earlier tightly controlled rhyming stanzas to experimenting with more open structures and rhythmically flexible lines. In this volume, however, Rich is not talking only about discrimination against women but also against the *feminine,* which she perceives as the "nurturing qualities in all people—whatever their sex." (Jong 172) Her vision is the creation of a humanity that will not glorify the chasm between male and female, but heal it. The drive to self-knowledge is not only a search for identity but part of her refusal of the self-destructiveness of a patriarchal culture. Rich's concept of patriarchy is not simplistic and does not imply only the tracing of descent through the father, but is also seen as:

> Any kind of group or organization in which males hold dominant power and determine what part females shall and shall not play and in which capabilities assigned to women are relegated generally to the mystical and aesthetic and excluded from the practical and political realms. (*ARP* 101)

She envisions an America and a world at large "beyond divisive polarities including the sexual" as Barbara and Albert Gelpi suggest (*ARP* XI). She is concerned about the "collective loss and fragmentation suffered by human beings in the denial and suppression of the *feminine*." (*ARP* 99, my italics) She believes with Jung's disciple Eric Newman, who wrote in 1952 in his introduction to *The Great Mother*, that the "problem of the Feminine has equal importance for the psychologist of culture, who realizes that the peril of present-day mankind springs in large part from the one-sidedly patriarchal development of the male intellectual consciousness, which is no longer kept in balance by the matriarchal world of the psyche." (*ARP* 99)

Rich is curious and expectant about the future of masculine consciousness as well and appeals to men to be kinder to themselves by recognizing and not struggling against their own subjective natures. As she writes in a poem, 'For the Dead':

> I dreamed I called you on the telephone
> to say: *be kinder to yourself*
> but you were sick and would not answer.
> The waste of my love goes on this way
> trying to save you from yourself. (*ARP* 74)

She laments that man's inaccessibility is thus responsible for "The tragedy of sex," which:

> lies around us, a woodlot
> the axes are sharpened for . . . .
> A man's world. But finished.
> They themselves have sold it to the machines. (*ARP* 62)

Rich's "visionary androgyne," to use Erica Jong's expression, will not only be the bisexual artist, but anyone concerned with saving the world. Even now, at the end of the twentieth century and the beginning of the twenty-first, Rich believes that the only way change can come about is "through the leadership of women" (Rothschild 5). *Snapshots* helped Rich break free from traditional taboos and the elaborate form and prosody of her earlier poetry that had limited the range of her creative expression. The volumes that followed were marked increasingly by a progressive paradigmatic shift, a transition from the personal to the political. Both *Necessities of Life* and *Leaflets* were attempts to forge significant connections between personal conflict and cultural oppression and the larger social and political currents gathering force in the civil rights, the anti-war and the emergent women's movements. The poem "Nightbreak," written at the peak of the Vietnam War, when the horror had become unbearable and the poet was cracking up, is an angry probe into the whole experience of political intrusion. Rich connects the violence her own nation inflicts on helpless children in other parts of the world, with the violence she experiences as a woman acquainted with the pain of motherhood. This helps her to make connections between Vietnam napalmed every moment and the lover's bed. The poem can thus be seen as a searing investigation of sexual politics in the larger context of oppression and the power that infuses all movements for liberation:

> In the bed the pieces fly together
> and the rifts fill or else
> my body is a list of wounds
> symmetrically placed
> a village
> blown open by planes
> that did not finish the job. (*ARP* 44)

With each subsequent volume, Rich confirmed and radicalized her fusion of political commitment and poetic vision, although her strongest allegiance was still given to the women's movement and the mobilization of this great force toward liberation. This is an experience she writes about trenchantly in her prose collection *Blood, Bread and Poetry:*

> Breaking the mental barrier that separated private from public life felt in itself like an enormous surge towards liberation. For a woman thus engaged, every aspect of her life was on the lines. We began naming and acting on issues we had been told were trivial, unworthy of mention: rape by husbands or lovers; the boss's hand groping the employee's breast, the woman beaten in her home, with no place to go, the woman sterilized when she sought an abortion; the lesbian penalized for her private life by loss of her child, her lease, her job. We pointed out that woman's unpaid work in the home is central to every economy, capitalist or socialist. And in the crossover between personal and political, we were pushing at the limits of experience reflected in literature, certainly in poetry. (181-82)

The private and the political thus ceased to exist in opposition and came to be perceived as complementary spheres in the process of an ever expanding and evolving consciousness.

The poems of *A Will to Change*, in which psychological and political revolutions continue to be perceived as interdependent, chronicle Rich's increasing rage at the denigration of women and continue to explore women's efforts to redefine their own reality. The title poem declares that individually and collectively we need not merely the will to exist, but more vitally, the will to change. At this stage poetry and patriarchy became a major engagement with Rich, who was well aware of the challenges women writers in the past had been confronted with. Interestingly enough, it is no accident that the publication of this volume coincided with her decision to end her seventeen-year-old marriage and even won her the Shelley Memorial Award for Poetry. From the masculinist point of view, the very nature of lyric poetry is inherently incompatible with the nature and essence of femaleness and a "woman poet is a contradiction in terms" suggest Sandra Gilbert and Susan Gubar (28). While commenting on a critical obsession with fulfillment, they cite the example of John Crowe Ransom and John Cody's critical assessment of Emily Dickinson's poetry. While one traces her creativity to the consummation of romance, the other attributes of her art to its "tormenting" absence. Neither "imagines that poetry itself could possibly constitute a woman's fulfillment. On the contrary, both assume that the art of a woman poet must in some sense arise from romantic feelings" (Gilbert and Gubar 30). The obvious implication is that when women's poetry has been praised, it has been so for its "femininity." *Unromantic* and *unfeminine* political verse is considered the work of perversity and insanity. Rich too echoes the same idea, substantiating it through the example of Marianne Moore who happened to be the most admired among the early women poets, on account of her "maidenly, elegant, intellectual, *discreet*" poetry" (*ARP* 94). It is towards the death of this stereotypical, mythic, angelic woman poet that Rich works. By becoming her own heroine and her own midwife, she seeks to bring forth her own monstrous being. This, says Rich, is not "loss of some fragile 'feminine' quality jeopardized by excellence in reasoning and analysis." It is a "consciousness of self as Other, which Simone de Beauvoir describes as that being towards whom man often feels fear, guilt, hostility and about whom he weaves his least defensible theories" (*ARP* 102-3). This "woman in the shape of a monster/a monster in the shape of a woman" (*ARP* 45) in her opinion, would have the potential for the most genuinely radical thought, questioning and action. As she says in her poem, "I Dream I'm the Death of Orpheus":

> A woman with certain mission
> which if obeyed to the letter will leave her intact.
> A woman with the nerves of a panther
> a woman with contacts among Hell's Angels
> a woman feeling the fullness of her powers
> at the precise moment when she must not use them
> a woman sworn to lucidity
> who sees through the mayhem, the smoky fires
> of these underground streets
> her dead poet learning to walk backward against the wind
> on the wrong side of the mirror. (*ARP* 50-51)

Rich is also concerned and disturbed over the way women have been opposed and their activities systematically devalued. Her poem 'Planetarium" (*ARP* 45), is a tribute to the astronomer Caroline Hershel (1750-1848), who discovered eight comets but whose accomplishments were eclipsed by the fame of her brother William. Emphasizing the difference between womanhood as it is and as it should be, she laments the mediocrity, self-indulgence, lack of will and discipline that results from sexual passivity, male domination and a nurturing maternal love. This romantic myth is questioned by Rich and other women poets, caught in the double bind of a split between their imagination and their real life-styles, their vocation and their gender. This whole process, which is seen as a choice between love (womanly, altruistic, maternal) and egotism (the force that is directed by men into creation, ambition, achievement often at the cost of others), needs to be re-visioned and redefined. Women cannot continue to be "primarily mothers and muses for men" (*ARP* 98) she states. If women are to survive the damaging effects of the dominant culture they must overcome:

> Self-trivialization, contempt for women, misplaced compassion, addiction (to love, to depression, to male approval); if we purge ourselves of this quadruple poison, we would have minds and bodies poised for the act of survival and rebuilding. (*LSS* 122-23)

In her book *Of Woman Born: Motherhood as Experience and Institution* (1986), Rich discusses motherhood as it now is and as it should be. She distinguishes between motherhood's potential and motherhood as an institution defined and ruled by the weight of an entire culture. Denying at the very outset, the existence of the nurturing instinct as a special female strength, she cautions against promoting this myth for creating a new regime, for that is a ploy, which could be a trap. In her book on second-wave feminism, Judith Evans rightly suggests that Rich does not believe there is anything "natural about the entire complex that is motherhood now, nor is there anything innate about the emotion involved" (85). Rich's inference is that we "learn . . . those qualities . . . patience, self-sacrifice, the willingness to repeat endlessly the small routine chores of socializing a human being," together with a fierce mixture of "love and violence by which a mother could kill for her child" (Evans 84). And yet powerless in a patriarchy, woman's powerlessness could very likely have a cascading effect that would turn a beneficent female principle into a self-destructive tendency by which, she could kill the child herself. "In a very non-violent way people can be so physically damaging to other people that they *are* violent," says Rich (*ARP* 106). Motherhood gives woman, power, but female power brings male retaliation and dislike. Motherhood so molded and stemming from patriarchal control, hence is the major source of women's inequality and denies to them its "most powerful" and most "fearful aspect authentic love." Institutionalized motherhood built on a series of self-denials, then, is "a poisoned chalice" (Evans 84). Rich's own experiences as a young wife and mother had actually prompted attempts to understand and analyze the historical and cultural contexts of women's lives, in the hope of arriving at a comprehensive view of the relationship between gender, social values and economic reality. Her personal anger over the circumstances of her own life had thus, charged her poetic and social vision as embodied in the public and historical dimensions of female experience, regardless of class, race or nationality.

As her understanding of patriarchy grew, Rich gradually came to believe that no individual could afford to ignore either the personal or the political scope of cultural solipsism. In fact, the very distinction between the personal and political might be nothing more than an illusion. 'Tear Gas' announces:

> The will to change begins in the body not in
> the mind.
> My politics is in my body, accruing and expanding
> with every
> act of resistance and each of my failures. (*CEP* 420)

The subjective, physical self thus became the focus for profound political change. A woman's need, consequently, was to assert control over her own destiny, physical and cultural, for which she required:

> a language to hear myself with
> to see myself in
> a language like pigment released on the board
> blood-black, sexual green, reds
> veined with contradictions
> bursting under pressure from the tube
> staining the old grain of wood. (*CEP* 420-21)

Rich had realized however, that the language for change was inadequate and it would be years before women could find the images they needed for this expression. Nonetheless, she was aware that she was now moving "toward a place where we can no longer be together" as men and women.

On receiving the National Book Award in 1974 for her volume *Diving into the Wreck,* Rich rejected the award in her individual capacity but accepted it in the name of all women:

> whose voices go unheard in a patriarchal world and in the name of those who like us, have been tolerated as token women in this culture, often at great cost and in great pain.

The statement written jointly with Audre Lorde and Alice Walker, was a symbolic refusal of the "terms of patriarchal competition," even while the occasion was dedicated to:

> the struggle for self determination of all women, of every color, identification or deprived class . . . the women who will understand what we are doing here and those who will not understand yet; the silent women whose voices have been denied us, the articulate women who have given us strength to do our work. (*ARP* 204)

Rich thus committed herself on this occasion, to the ideal of co-operation among women, by emphasizing the need for a shared female identity that transcended race, class, and nationality. This she believed, would be the common platform from which, an effective political vision could grow. Alongside, the poet also cautioned against the subversive nature of the patriarchal myth of the token woman which, flattering as it may be, could be divisive and destructive, setting woman against woman and woman against herself. Such women, she warned, would be romanticized and tolerated as long as "their words and actions didn't threaten [men's] privilege of tolerating or rejecting [women] according to *their* ideas of what a special woman ought to be." (*ARP* 93)

Diving into the Wreck, was a phenomenal work that engaged Rich's most complex use of the image of rebirth and in which, she took the bold step of articulating her political vision in uncompromising feminist terms. The volume thus established her as a major voice in the women's movement. Like Emily Dickinson before her, Rich too had turned to the community of women to sustain her as a writer and as a woman, but her vision transcended Dickinson's close-knit circle of friends to include women as a national, even transnational force. In the late Sixties and early Seventies, her political activism had evolved into a major concern for women's issues and a love for women, as is quite evident from her poem 'The Phenomenology of Anger':

> *The only real love I have ever felt*
> *was for children and other women*
> *Everything else was lust, pity,*
> *Self-hatred, pity, lust.*
> This is a woman's confession. (*ARP* 71)

Rich's poetry at this stage, addressed itself to an identity politics, which was concerned less with how women had been spoken of, shown to be and more with the question of *how* we could speak for them, show them. Her empathy however, was not reserved for women alone but was also extended to the revolutionary male as her 1968 poem "To Franz Fanon," the Algerian psychiatrist and revolutionary, shows. She was forceful in her insistence that "it is important for oppressed people to fight back in order to gain selfhood and identity." (Martin 182) However, she was to realize later, that revolutionary men too were as sexist as traditional patriarchs were and it was necessary for women to determine their own political vision. In the poems of *Diving into the Wreck*, Rich had envisioned an alternative culture, practically and metaphorically woman-centered. Repudiating patriarchal premises, the poet had sought at this stage, a sense of personal integrity based on the acceptance of shared female experience—an integrity that would go on to nurture a community capable of transforming the linguistic, institutional and mythological premises of patriarchy. *A Will to Change* and *Diving into the Wreck*, were both cathartic volumes that demonstrated a progressive coming to power in the "desolation patriarchy enacts on literal and psychic landscape." (Pope 3) *Diving into the Wreck* thus reflected successively, the poet's determination to write directly and overtly of woman, not as a victim but as a survivor and closed significantly with her poem 'From a Survivor,' in which she bid final farewell to a marriage of pretence:

> I don't know who we thought we were
> that our personalities
> could resist the failures of the race . . . .
> Like everybody else, we thought of ourselves as
> special

However, she writes:

> you are wastefully dead
> who might have made the leap
> we talked, too late, of making
>
> which I have now
> not as a leap
> but a succession of brief, amazing movements
>
> each one making possible the next. (*ARP* 74-75)

The opening poem of the volume 'Trying to Talk with a Man,' effectively conveys the dread of a failing marriage, by equaling it to the dangers and dread of cultural annihilation associated with nuclear destruction. The conversation, ironically enough, takes place in a desert landscape. Rich skillfully integrates both states by juxtaposing domestic imagery against the sterile landscape of a Nevada test site, conveying powerfully thereby, the sense of futility, despair and loss linked with both. Connecting the problem of survival with the problem of communication, she states ruefully:

> Out here I feel more helpless
> with you than without you, . . .
> we talk of people caring for each other
> in emergencies—laceration, thirst—
> but you look at me like an emergency.

Both sites regrettably, seem bombed beyond reclamation:

> Your dry heat feels like power
> your eyes are stars of different magnitude

they reflect lights that spell out: EXIT
when you get up and pace the floor. (*ARP* 58-59)

By intricately linking gender relations and the "condemned" landscape of modern civilization, Rich becomes a vehicle of historical awareness and "alters our sense of both irreversibly" as John Gery significantly suggests (5).

Rich shares the cultural/radical feminist's hope for change through recognition of a beneficent female principle and rejects a patriarchal order that threatens women and children. She advocates a liberation of this female principle, which she defined as "the mother in all women and the woman in some men," from the confines of all "male-induced notions of where the female principle is valid or where it is not." (*ARP* 104-5) She is different however, from the stereotypical feminist essentialist, in her advocacy of women's active participation in scientific disciplines, especially those relevant to reproductive change. Closely linked with the idea of motherhood and a women's culture is Rich's proposal that all women are lesbians in that, like motherhood, the lesbian experience too is a profoundly *female* experience and insofar as they want to identify with other women. Nonetheless, this does not necessarily imply that they must be lesbians in the limited clinically identified sense. For Rich, compulsory heterosexuality as it exists today maintains subordination, as it demands women's identification with men. In a way women lead double lives because lesbianism is hidden/written away from them. So strong is the institution that it is seldom asked why the mother-daughter bond does not lead to identification with women instead?

In a position paper entitled "The Woman-Identified Woman," published in 1972 by a collective of lesbian feminists who called themselves Radicalesbians, the lesbian has been identified as "the rage of all women condensed to the point of explosion" (*VBF* 162). In the late sixties, lesbians had begun to pressure The National Organization for Women founded by Betty Friedan in 1966, to support their struggle for human rights.

Robin Morgan, an active lesbian feminist, poet and novelist, had charged Friedan and her followers with adopting anti-lesbian sentiments in the interest of producing a respectable public image for feminism. Resultantly in 1971, NOW passed a resolution affirming a woman's right "to define and express her own sexuality" and acknowledged that the "oppression of lesbians [was] a legitimate concern of feminism" (*VBF* 162). However, while some 'straight' feminists afraid of being labeled as dykes dissociated themselves from the movement, others became lesbians by choice for they saw lesbianism as a form of active feminism. Rich's 1986 essay, "Compulsory Heterosexuality and Lesbian Existence," then, is an elaborate defense of a lesbian continuum even while it sets out to right some misconceived notions and unravel the politics of lesbian identifications. Rich endorses the basic argument of Radicalesbians: "lesbian is one of the categories by which men have divided up humanity." It is a tool "to frighten a woman into a less militant stand, keep her separate from her sisters, keep her from giving primacy to anything other than men and family" and to ensure thereby "control by male culture." (*VBF* 164-65) Rich, too, sees compulsory heterosexuality as an ideology, a "lie" foisted on women "through which lesbian existence is perceived on a scale ranging from deviant to abhorrent or simply rendered invisible." (*VBF* 312) This is evident not only from the several texts, which assume women's total erotic and sexual orientation as well as loyalty towards men, but also from every conversation or relationship over which it hovers. Lesbians are projected as victims of misandry, misogamy and "phallic envy," while lesbianism is seen as the enactment of women's bitterness against men. Rich is as concerned with affecting a disengagement from male-defined response patterns that invalidate women's sexual preference for other women, as she is with the "virtual or total neglect of lesbian existence" from male and more so from feminist scholarship. Lesbians have been involved with the women's movement from its inception, yet they have encountered antagonism where they least expected it-in the feminist family itself. Some feminists even felt that the movement would hurt the women's cause. As such, Rich suggests that a "feminist critique of compulsory heterosexual orientation for women is long overdue," in order to "understand the societal forces which wrench women's emotional and erotic energies away from themselves and other women and from woman-identified values" (*VBF* 312-13). She sees lesbianism as a precarious solidarity to gender. She argues that a forcibly or subliminally imposed heterosexual "preference" through which men deny women their sexuality, is more significant and easily recognizable among a pervasive cluster of forces ranging from physical brutality to control of consciousness by which, men exercise control over women. She identifies lesbianism as "woman identified experience, not simply the fact that a woman has had a consciously desired genital sexual experience with another woman." (*VBF* 317) It is the male grid, the male "class-identification system that defines all females in sexual relation to some other category of people" and as potential sex objects, that lays a "surrogate male role on the lesbian." (Radicalesbians 164) Rich perceives lesbianism as female bonding, an extending and receiving of support against male tyranny and the "sharing of a rich inner life." (317) It can be seen as a viable and authentic way of understanding a central fact of the history and psychology of female experience. It implies the breaking of a taboo, the rejection of a compulsory way of life and more importantly of man's right of access to women. Rich interprets eroticism in female terms as a diffuse energy "unconfined to any single part of the body or solely to the body itself." Quoting from the African-American lesbian poet Audre Lorde's essay "Uses of the Erotic: The Erotic as Power," she substantiates her perception of female eroticism as being omnipresent. Lorde posits that the erotic is the core of the self, it is the power of love that arises from the self's deepest, non-rational knowledge and female eroticism lies in "the sharing of joy whether physical, emotional, psychic." Empowerment, Lorde suggests, lies in the sharing of work "which makes us less willing to accept powerlessness, or those other supplied states of being which are not native to me, such as resignation, despair, self-effacement, depression, self-denial" (*VBF* 319). Rich discerns lesbianism in marriage resisters like Emily Dickinson the *nineteenth century white woman* genius and Zora Neil Hurston the *twentieth century Black woman* genius, also. While the former lived "self-convicted" in her father's home and wrote passionate letters to her sister-in-law Susan Gilbert, Hurston survived two broken marriages and her only sustaining relationships were with women, beginning with her mother. Both women understood that women must be one another's allies, mentors and comforters in the female struggle for survival and resistance against already offered clichés. Both enjoyed intellectual companionship with men but "fascination" and sustenance came from their relationships with women. "WOMAN IDENTIFICATION IS A SOURCE OF POWER" and liberation, stresses Rich. Compulsory heterosexuality, which was named as one of the 'crimes against women' by the Brussels International Tribunal on Crimes against Women' in 1976, equals psychological entrapment and blocked options. It is an incalculable loss of power through the dissimulation and disintegration that women suffer under pressure. In the face of institutionalized heterosexuality, Rich perceives in the act of choosing a female partner, "a *nascent* feminist political content." However, "for lesbian existence to realize this political content in an ultimately liberating form, the erotic choice must deepen and expand into conscious woman identification—into lesbian feminism." (324) Lesbianism is thus seen as an empathy for and soli darity to gender not simply because women suffer under homophobia as a stigmatized group, but also because they are extremely creative, active and have a particular understanding of the human condition. Nonetheless, Rich does not preclude heterosexual relationships and even acknowledges the qualitative difference of experience in individual cases and diversified group situations of the least oppressive ones. Yet, she is skeptical about the collective power of such relationships to determine the meaning and place of sexuality in women's lives, because of the absence of choice. The matter of choice still remains an unacknowledged absence and relatively successful heterosexual relationships are largely dependent on chance and luck. She thus advocates an in-depth understanding of the politics of different-sex alliances to "undo the power men everywhere wield over women." (326)

Rich's political awareness and critique of conventional male-female identities, on which so much of western poetry is based, has enabled her to come out sexually. For her lesbianism, then, forms part of a much wider conversation about justice, power and citizenship. She concentrates on the lived experience of women in the hope that feminine consciousness can foster an increasingly democratic and egalitarian society. At the structural center of the volume *The Dream of a Common Language* (1978), are "Twenty-One Love Poems," that are a tender and sensuous celebration of lesbian relationships and the power of love, especially the love of women for women, in reconstituting the world. Apart from "The Floating Poem Unnumbered," which is Rich's most erotic poem to date—"Your body/will haunt mine" (*DCL* 32)—the poems of this volume are extraordinary, in that they are not narrowed but expanded by their focus, because they transcend sex. They break the silences that smother lesbian sexuality, relationships and identity and resist thereby, a co-optation into the heterosexual system that they challenge. These poems reflect a strong desire to break free of a public history that ascribes lesbian deviance:

> Whenever in the city
> sirens flicker
> with pornography . . .
> We also have to walk. (*DCL* 25)

Aware of the struggles in daily life that such relationships are likely to encounter, Rich also knows that private attachments cannot exist in isolation and must subsist in the contexts of a wider public life:

> If I could let you know
> two women together is a work
> nothing in civilization has made simple
> two people together is a work
> heroic in its ordinariness. (*DCL* 35)

These poems then, "rely on the reader's recognizing the ideologies associated with heterosexuality and conventional ways of reading against which [they] position themselves." (Templeton 3) The volume, on the whole, presents a more hopeful vision of community among women, through the creation of positive public images of women, to counteract masculinist projections of subjection of the female mind and objectification of the female body. Rich's "poetics of transgression," thus, becomes "a source of truth," as Joan Feit Diehl correctly contends. *The Dream of a Common Language* is divided into three sections, each with a different focus. While the poems of the first section, 'Power,' are concerned with the outstanding achievements of individual women, they reflect Rich's preference for women in positions of power even as they extend her vision of women's capabilities. The second section 'Origins and History of Consciousness,' composed over a period of two years, projects images of a women no longer cooped and confined by:

> the hunter
> the trapper
> the wardens of the mind

These liberated women live in a community where:

> No one sleeps . . . without
> the dream of a common language. (*DCL* 8)

The complexities of this womanpower are inherent in the story of Nobel Laureate Marie Curie, the uncommon woman scientist who won wide patriarchal acclaim and endorsement. Rich underscores the seductive and destructive nature of patriarchal competitiveness that tokenizes women and lures them away from the dream of a common language. However, she indicts the killer and not the achiever who sacrificed self for the world and who could be killed by the destructive power of her own discovery, uranium—a source of energy and death—because she did not know how to handle power:

> She died a famous woman denying
> her wounds
> denying
> her wounds came from the same source as
> her power. (*DCL* 3)

The poems of this section are not only a celebration of woman-power, but also a record of heroic resilience because it is a history of survivors in the face of counter-forces against which the passion for survival prevailed. The need for female collectivity and power is explored in the third section 'Not Somewhere Else, But Here' and the central metaphor of the poem 'Natural Resources' is that of a miner who explores the fissures of the female mind for psychological excavations. The poet calls upon the nurturing power of women here, "to help deliver the world' and casts her lot with those:

> who age after age, perversely,
> with no extraordinary power,
> reconstitute the world. (*DCL* 67)

The final poem of the volume, 'Transcendental Etude,' is the vision of a woman whose energies are balanced between the self and its historical time and place. She is a woman capable of self-transformation, a woman with a negative capability that enables her to become:

> now the shard of broken glass
> slicing light in a corner, dangerous
> to flesh, now the plentiful, soft leaf
> that wrapped round the throbbing finger soothes,
> the wound

> and now the stone foundation, rockshelf further
> forming underneath everything that grows. (*DCL* 77)

Rich's next volume, *A Wild Patience Has Taken Me This Far* (1981), continues to celebrate the accomplishments of women and to urge women to re-vision, to be disloyal to the patriarchal lie. Her poem 'Culture and Anarchy,' which borrows its title from Matthew Arnold's 1869 collection of essays, once again echoes the poet's engagement with the idea of being "nourished not bound by ideas." Past and present are thus brought together in the comprehensive framework of female community and vision. The poem includes excerpts from the diaries, letters, memoirs, essays, and speeches of Suffragists like Susan Brownell Anthony, Jane Addams, Elizabeth Barrett Browning, Ida Huston Harper and Elizabeth Cady Stanton set in unbroken iambic pentameter, to convey a powerful sense of the vigor of their vision. Sorority, which lies at the heart of the poem, is conveyed through the strong bonds between Susan Anthony and Cady Stanton, Elizabeth Barrett Browning and Mary Russell Mitford, Emily and Charlotte Bronte, Adrienne Rich and Michelle Cliff. Rich even incorporates a selection of one of Stanton's letters to Anthony to contrast the shared love and proximity of these women with patriarchal controls ranging from social exclusion to rape:

> I should miss you more than any other
> living being from this earth . . .
> Yes, our work is one,
> we are one in aim and sympathy
> and we should be together. (*WP* 15)

In an eight-part poem, 'Turning the Wheel,' which concludes the volume, Rich rejects the exemption from routine that romanticism exalts and posits instead, a liberation that underscores the importance of choice, to sustain life on the basis of women's actual, lived experience:

> So long as you want her faceless, without smell

> or voice . . .
> so long as she does not have her own peculiar
> face, . . .
> so long as you try to simplify her meaning
> so long as she simply *symbolizes* power
> she is kept helpless and conventional. (*WP* 56)

The message Rich wishes to convey through these poems then, is contained in the very title of a 1977 essay entitled, "The Meaning of Our Love for Women is What We Have Constantly to Expand."

Rich's later volumes, *The Fact of a Doorframe* (1984), and *Your Native Land Your Life* (1986), suggest that she had subjected her separatism to extensive reconsideration and had resultantly moved closer to the cultural mainstream. *Time's Power* (1989) *and An Atlas of a Difficult World* (*1991*) continue the process of re-visioning and confirm as well as radicalize her fusion of political commitment and poetic vision. *Dark Fields of the Republic* (*1995*), *Midnight Salvage* (*1999*) *and Fox: Poems 1998-2000* (2001), all continue to alternate her sights between her personal life and the larger social issues she has espoused. She has remained remarkably free of long-term fixations on any particular 'alternative' approach and has committed herself to writing poetry that will be catalytic to social change. In prophesying a community of women and of female energy free from patriarchal repression, she envisions:

> The transformation of society and our relation to all life . . . It goes far beyond any struggle for civil liberties or equal rights—necessary as those struggles continue to be. In its deepest, most inclusive form it is an inevitable process by which women will claim our primary and central vision in shaping the future. (*LSS* 226)

Rich has continued to grow, shed her skin and evolve at every stage of her life. Her effort has been to create social and artistic forms that express women's actual experience and her poetic vision lies in the exploration of new human and communal possibilities. Her journey through growing stages of personal and political awareness has generated a whole body of criticism, for perhaps somewhere along the line she may have stepped out of the terse and formal territory of poetry into the dangerous precincts of polemics, but never has her poetry degenerated into propaganda. She projects her art as a force within social life, a power that celebrates woman's capacity to integrate politics and self-reflexivity with actual speech. However, coming to terms with the excesses of her programmatic work, she makes that awareness an index of the values one can create as a political poet.

In 'Dedications,' the last section of the poem 'An Atlas of the Difficult World,' which she was writing during and after the Gulf war, she writes:

> I know you are reading this poem listening for something,
> torn between bitterness and hope
> turning back once again to the task you cannot refuse
> I know you are reading this poem because there is nothing
> else left to read
> There where you have landed, stripped as you are.

Rich's difficult world is the United States of America. As she explains in a conversation with Bill Moyers, the poem which in its entirety "reflects the condition of my country," was written "consciously as a citizen poet, looking at the geography, the history, the peoples of my country. . . . 'Dedications' came to me as a way of creating a personal dialogue with many different kinds of readers who might have read this whole poem and connected with it here and there." (345) The entire thirteen-part poem is addressed to the citizen who strives for transparency in her/his life and country. Cataloguing several readers in diverse situations both at home and at work, she establishes an immediate sense of fellowship with them as individuals and as a "pan of collectivity." Through the poem she enters into a dialogical relationship with her community in mutual concern, understanding, need and desire. The voices in the poem are not all either the poet's or of women but those of a community fully awake to the horrors of their reality and affiliated in general anxiety and solicitude. The poem is thus a deconstruction of the myth of Sisyphus in the collaborative effort of the poet and her community, which has been "stripped" of so much of what was promised and hoped for, to build stronger foundations of democracy. Rich believes with other like-minded poets of the fraternity, that the writer must carry a heavy burden of social responsibility, for poetry can never cease to matter.

The epigraph to this essay is taken from her volume *Dark Fields of the Republic*, which deals in part with government and art and reflects Rich's faith that power inheres in the word. Referring to these lines, she tells Michael Klein in a June 1999 interview for *The Boston Phoenix*, that she was responding in the poem, to Medbh McGuckian an Irish poet who she admires greatly. McGuckian was writing from Belfast during the war and Rich had responded: "on the level of what it means to be working in a language, in a time or situation when it feels that language can do so little." Even though in the given reality, being a writer seems so illogical, Rich still believes in the power of committed and energetic poetry to jostle, to disturb, to enrapture and to set into motion, the whole process of transformation. "Poetry can add its grain to an accumulation of consciousness against the idea that there is no alternative" in today's world of mayhem and capitalism, she believes. Her work comes from an intense desire for connection and "art and literature have given so many people the relief of being connected," she tells Klein. If *Midnight Salvage* as a volume, repudiates rather than ratifies the idea that there is no alternative by reflecting things as they are rather than as they could be, it is a conscious strategy. It is a sort of electromagnetic therapy that could throw up several options several possibilities of what the poet, and by extension we, could salvage from a world enrivened by an insane hunger for material power and territorial expansion, on the threshold of a new century. In a sterile landscape vitiated by gross violations of human rights, in the face of global disaster and devastation, she believes that poetry, the "awful bridge rising over naked air," can provide solace and make connections. As she writes in 'Victory,' a simultaneously horrifying and beautiful poem from her most recent volume *Fox: Poems 1998-2000*:

> In coldest Europe   end of that war
> frozen domes   iron railings frozen   stoves
>   lit in the streets
> memory banks of cold
>
> the Nike of Smothrace
> on a staircase   wings in blazing
> backdraft   said to me
> : : to everyone she met
>   *Displaced, amputated, never discount me.*
>   Victory
>   indented in disaster   striding
>   at the head of stairs.

Works Cited

da Costa, Paulo. "Interview with Adrienne Rich." *Samsara Quarterly* 2001. Text downloaded from www.english.uiuc.edu/maps/poets/m_r/ rich /onlineints.htm. 5-8.

Diehl, Joan Fiet. "'Cartographies of Silence': Rich's Common Language and the Woman Poet." *Feminist Studies*. Fall 1980.

Du Plessis, Rachael Blau. 1986. *Hilda Doolittle: The Career of that Struggle*. Brighton: Harvester Press. Hereafter cited as *HD*.

______. 1985. *Writing beyond the Ending: Narrative Strategies of Twentieth Century Woman Writers*. Bloomington: Indiana Univ. Press. Hereafter cited as *WBE*.

Evans, Judith. 1995. *An Introduction to Second-Wave Feminism*. London: Sage.

Gelpi, Barbara and Albert. Ed. 1975. *Adrienne Rich's Poetry*. New York: W.W. Norton. Hereafter cited as *ARP*.

______. Ed. 1979. *Adrienne Rich's Poetry and Prose: A Norton Critical Edition*. New York: Norton. Hereafter cited as *ARP & P*.

Gery, John. 1996. *Ways of Nothingness: Nuclear Annihilation and Contemporary American Poetry*. Florida: Board of Regents. Excerpt downloaded from www.english.uiuc.edu/maps/poets/m_r/rich/trying.htm.

Gilbert, Sandra and Gubar, Susan. "Women Poets" *Literature in the Modern World: Critical Essays and Documents*. Ed. Denis Walder. 1990. New Delhi: OUP. 27-33.

Jong, Erica. "Visionary Anger" *Adrienne Rich's Poetry*. 171-74.

Keyes, Claire. 1986. *The Aesthetics of Power: The Poetry of Adrienne Rich.* Athens: The University of Georgia.

Klein, Michael. "A Rich Life: Adrienne Rich on Poetry, Politics and Personal Revelation." *The Boston Phoenix*. June 1999.

Lorde, Audre. 1984. "Poetry is Not a Luxury." *Sister Outsider: Essays and Speeches*. Trumansburg. New York: Crossing Press.

______. "Uses of the Erotic: The Erotic as Power." *Sister Outsider*.

Martin, Wendy. 1984. *An American Triptych: Ann Bradstreet, Emily Dickinson, Adrienne Rich.* Chapel Hill: Univ. of North Carolina Press. Hereafter cited as *AAT*.

______. "From Patriarchy to the Female Principle." *Adrienne Rich's Poetry*. 172-89.

Moyers, Bill. 1995. "Conversations with Adrienne Rich" *The Language of Life: A Festival of Poets*. New York: Doubleday. 335-53.

Nelson, Cary. 1981. *Our Last First Poets: Vision and History in Contemporary American Poetry.* Urbana: Univ. of Illinois Press.

Pope, Deborah. 1995. "Rich's Life and Career." *The Oxford Companion to Women's Writing in the United States*. New York: OUP.

Prince, Ruth EC "The Possibilities of an Engaged Art: An Interview with Adrienne Rich" *Radcliffe Quarterly*. Fall 1998.

Radicalesbians. "The Woman-Identified Woman." *The Vintage Book of Feminism*. 160-167.

Rich, Adrienne. 2001. *Fox: Poems 1998-2000*. New York: W.W. Norton. Hereafter cited as *FP*.

______. 1999. *Midnight Salvage: Poems 1995-1998*. New York: W.W. Norton. Hereafter cited as *MS*.

______.1995. *Dark Fields of the Republic: Poems 1991-1995*. New York: W.W. Norton. Hereafter cited as *DFR*.

______.1993. *Collected Early Poems*. New York: W.W. Norton. Hereafter cited as *CEP*.

______. 1991. *An Atlas of the Difficult World: Poems 1988-1991*. New York: W.W. Norton. Hereafter cited as *ADW*.

______. 1986. *Your Native Land Your Life: Poems*. New York: W.W. Norton. Hereafter cited as *YNL*.

______.1984. *The Fact of a Doorframe: Poems Selected and New 1950-1984*. New York: W.W. Norton. Hereafter cited as *FD*.

______. 1981. *A Wild Patience Has Taken Me Thus Far: Poems 1978-1981*. New York: W.W. Norton. Hereafter cited as *WP*.

______.1978. *The Dream of a Common Language: Poems 1974-1977*. New York: W.W. Norton. Hereafter cited as *DCL*.

______. 1973. *Diving into the Wreck: Poems 1971-1972*. New York: W.W. Norton. Hereafter cited as *DW*.

______. 1973. *The Will to Change: Poems 1968-1970*. New York: W.W. Norton. Hereafter cited as *WC*.

______. 1972. *Leaflets: Poems 1965-1968*. New York: W.W. Norton. Hereafter cited as *L*.

______. 1966. *Necessities of Life: Poems 1962-1965*. New York: W.W. Norton Hereafter cited as *NL*.

______. 1963. *Snapshots of a Daughter-in-Law: Poems 1954-1962*. New York: Harper and Row. Hereafter cited as *SDL*.

______. 1951. *A Change of World*. New Haven: Yale Univ. Press. Hereafter cited as *CW*.

______. 2001. *Arts of the Possible: Essays and Conversations*. New York: W.W. Norton:

______. 1993. *What is Found There: Notebooks on Poetry and Politics*. New York: W.W. Norton.

______. 1986. *Blood, Bread and Poetry: Selected Prose 1975-1985*. New York: W.W. Norton. Hereafter cited as *BBP*.

______. 1979. *On Lies, Secrets and Silence: Selected Prose 1966-1978*. New York: W.W. Norton. Hereafter cited as *LSS*.

______. 1976. *Of Woman Born: Motherhood as Experience and Institution*. New York: W.W. Norton. Hereafter cited as *OWB*.

______. "Credo of a Passionate Skeptic." *Los Angeles Times*. Sunday, March 11, 2001. Hereafter cited as *LA Times*.

______. "Why I Refused the National Medal For the Arts." *Los Angeles Times Book Section*. August 3, 1997. Hereafter cited as *LA Times BS*.

______. Letter to Jane Alexander, Head, The National Endowment for the Arts. June3, 1997. Text downloaded from www.english.uiuc.edu/maps/poets/m_r/rich/onlineessays.htm.

______. "Defy the Space that Separates." *The Nation*, October 7, 1996.

______. "Three Conversations." *Adrienne Rich's Poetry.* 105-22.

______. "When we Dead Awaken: Writing as Revision." *Adrienne Rich's Poetry.* 90-98.

______. "The Anti-Feminist Woman." *Adrienne Rich's Poetry.* 99-105.

______. "Compulsory Heterosexuality and Lesbian Existence." *The Vintage Book of Feminism.* 311-26.

Rothschild, Mathew. "Adrienne Rich: I happen to think poetry makes a huge difference." *The Progressive.* 1994. 1-11. Text downloaded from www.english.uiuc.edu/maps/poets/m_r/rich/progressive.htm.

Schneir, Miriam. Ed. 1995. *The Vintage Book of Feminism.* New York: Vintage. Hereafter cited as *WBF.*

Simpson, Pat. Marchand, Michele and Freeman, Anitra. "Adrienne Rich: Standing at the Intersection of Art and Activism." *Real Change News.* April 19, 2001.

Templeton, Alice. 1994. *The Dream and the Dialogue.* Knoxville: The Univ. Press. Excerpt downloaded from www.english.uiuc.edu/maps/poets/m_r/rich/dedications.htm.

Tonks, Rosemary. "Cutting the Marble." *New York Review of Books.* October 4, 1973. 8-10.

Vendler, Helen. 1980. *Part of Nature, Part of the U.S.: Modern American Poetry.* Cambridge MA: Harvard Univ. Press.

Werner, Craig. 1988. *Adrienne Rich: The Poet and Her Critics.* Chicago: American Library Association.

Tradition and Skepticism: Mamta Kalia

Let us forget your death and mine
We have so much to remember
A comfortable home
Your air-conditioned office
Our quarter-dozen children
Your bank balance
. . . .
And all those engagements
Who cares for primal disappointments?

Mamta Kalia

Mamta Kalia's recent conversation with Eunice de Souza in the latter's book *Talking Poems: Conversations with Poets*, focuses on the problems that an "educated, liberated, outspoken individual who happens to be a woman" (59), has to face in the pursuit of her profession. That life for a woman writer, academic and housewife, all rolled into one, can be quite harried, hurried and worried is a fact no one would more readily agree with, than Kalia. Drawing a fine distinction between academic proposals and real-life situations, she concedes that even if you "equip yourself academically, professionally, you cannot hope others will move at the same pace." And this, she reiterates, "brings about a crisis in your attitude." (*TP* 61) With several awards under her cap including two for short stories, this bilingual writer says that she has "no transit problems" (*EDS* 18) between two diverse mediums and is as comfortable writing in English as she is in Hindi. She has even evolved her own distinct style, which is to be appreciated as much for its wit as for its thematic complexities. Her poetry marks a departure from the confessionalism of Kamala Das Surayya and moves toward a more confident idiom that is born out of a compulsive need to capture the ordinariness of an uneventful life. Her life she says, is packed with nothing but the "prosaic details" (*TP* 65) of "pending phone calls," "dirty linen," "a shaky mountain of books," a much needed hair wash" (*EDS* 22-23). With characteristic nonchalance, Kalia admits that she too is caught up like others before her, in the ubiquitous double bind of the woman writer. Straddling the two worlds of tradition and modernity, freedom and bondage, domesticity and professionalism, her creative graph has been wavering between "flashes and crashes," that is between periods of great inspirational vigor that can "erupt like a volcano" and of poetic lull in which "you lie low." (*TP* 66) This vacillation between two extreme states only helps underscore the poet's divided consciousness.

Author of five novels, seven short story collections, two one-act play collections, four novelettes in Hindi for children, besides editing three anthologies, Mamta Kalia has published just two volumes of poetry in English. Yet, she is recognized as an important member of the new generation poets whose works are distinguishable by the felicity with which they have incorporated and adapted traditional forms of imaginative expression, to the exigencies of an inherited English language. The relative ease with her medium and the down-to-earth realism with which she captures her mundane, middle-class existence, has helped initiate what Bruce King terms as "the present contemporary manner" (155). The writer herself acknowledges the fact that "in 1998 you cannot write in the manner of 1948. Today language is breaking down, diction is splitting up" (*TP* 58) and a stripping-down of style is essential to avoid dissonance with the contemporary reality of dot COM and bio data. And yet, there is a complexity and poignancy underlying the ironic wit and surface simplicity of her poems that arises out of a profound concern for the overlapping worlds of tradition and skepticism, collective responsibility and individual choice. This whole process is seen as a choice between womanly, maternal and altruistic love, and egotism, that is the force directed by men into creation, ambition and achievement, often at the cost of others. Much that she would have loved to, the poet has been unable to follow a full-time writing career, even though she confesses that she would "die on a wordless day." (*TP* 64) Hence she admits wryly, "I snapped myself into two bits. Like a pod. One bit was obeying, towing and rowing; the other raised its head well past midnight and scribbled away in diaries, on the back of envelopes, on office file covers. To this day this happens." (*TP* 59) The poet is anxious, but it is not so much the Bloomian anxiety of influence attributable to a stronger literary predecessor, as it is an apprehension about being able to write at all. Kalia worries "about an unfinished poem or story. I begin, I don't end. I leave stories midway, midstream, and midair," she concedes. (*TP* 64) This passionate concern for her poetic career is further compounded by her unease over the pain she might inflict in the pursuance of a full time artistic vocation, on her "fastidious husband," her two "non-studious sons," (*TP* 65) her friends and wizened old relatives whose:

> wrinkled hands, beaten faces and grey eyelashes
> Were all too much too real. (*EDS* 26)

Yet, even while working within normative parameters and mutually adjustable time schedules, which she pithily defines as "hurry and curry" (*TP* 64), her poetry provides ample evidence of the effort that goes into striking a tenuous balance between relational expectations and responsibilities and individual proclivities. "I like to write at a time when my feelings are at my fingertips, but all my routine jobs take away the fire," she confesses ruefully (*TP* 64). Like most women writers before her then, Kalia too is trapped in the dichotomy between her imagination and her real life-style, her vocation and her gender. Having to juggle several roles, she realizes that it is the creativity of the woman writer that is almost invariably relegated.

Kalia is as caught up with parodying inequitable human relationships as she is with exposing the hypocrisy of middle-class respectability and social issues concerning women. Her played-down persona, her crisp, terse wit and her colloquial idiom however, lend her poems a wry humor that makes the "enormous uncertainty of this universe" (*TP* 63) and the sordidness of life seem relatively bearable. Quite contrary to Chavan's contention that her "irony often becomes a mere substitute for anger and disgust signifying nothing" (75), her poetry which is free from sentimental pastiche, engages in a meaningful and dialogic relationship with the other:

> discussing our dislikes,
> sharing a few hatreds
> comparing notes on enemies. (*EDS* 22)

Unwilling to be treated as a decorative ornament, a member of a special-interest group handicapped by subordinate status, she states her wants unambiguously, demanding that she be recognized for her own worth:

> I want to throw away
> all my cosmetics
> I want to reveal
> real age. (22)

Born in Mathura, the now sixty-two years old Kalia was till recently the Principal of Mahila Seva Sadan Degree College in Allahabad. The place she says was so "politically charged" that you had to "peel off your ego to get along" and the only resource for survival was her "creativity at its biting best." (*TP* 63) This would probably account for the fine sense of balance in both, her personal as well as her professional life—a virtue that extends to her poetic articulations as well. After schooling in Delhi, Nagpur, Bombay and Pune, she earned a master's degree in English Literature from the University of Delhi in 1963. A regular broadcaster for Akashvani and Doordarshan, she is married to the noted Hindi writer Ravinder Kalia whom she met in 1965 at a seminar in Chandigarh. He was then an established writer, while she was still struggling and "breaking up within," (*TD* 58) to be heard. Her first volume of poetry *A Tribute to Papa and Other Poems* (1970), was followed by a second volume entitled *Poem'78* (1979) and both were published by the Writers' Workshop, Calcutta. In her conversation with de Souza, Kalia informs us that her father was a teacher and a scholar of Hindi and English while her uncle, the late Bharat Bhushan Aggarwal, was a prominent poet of the progressive movement. The younger of two siblings, she was the plain Jane while her sister Pratibha was the talented good looker of the family. The poet is curiously quiet about her mother who has been consigned to oblivion after finding brief mention in a poem 'Brat,' as a progenitor who has nothing to be proud of:

> Except for the comfort
> That I looked like Papa
> And not like the neighbour
> Who shared our bathroom. (24)

Kalia's father wanted her to be "different" and "superb." He compelled her to read certain "inevitable writers such as Bankim, Sharat, Tagore, Nehru, Gandhi and Bertrand Russell," she says (*TP* 62), even though her own interest lay in reading Donne, Blake, Eliot, Rilke, Frost, Auden and Dylan Thomas among other writers. This patriarch hovers over the title poem of her first volume, 'Tribute to Papa' (20-21), as a "gutless," "model man," "A sort of an ideal," who wanted to fulfill himself vicariously by dreaming the poet's dreams for her:

> You wanted me to be like you, Papa,
> Or like Rani Lakshmibai.
> You're not sure what greatness is
> you want me to be great. (20)

The poem takes on the narrative form of a song of abuse, which opens with a direct address to the father, enumerates a series of patriarchal vices particularly those that affect her and through a categorical declaration of her independence, suddenly and unexpectedly closes on a note of concern. This sudden turn at the close is quite possibly motivated by an awareness of the pain that is encountered in the process of snapping filial bonds and challenging social taboos. The poem is a powerful expose of middle-class hypocrisy and established relationships and offers a witty and sardonic comment on rampant corruption and established values. Its implicit irony and complex subtlety percolates through a deceptively explicit derision for the father, who could not even "wangle a cozy place in the world" and would not hesitate to "think of suicide," were his daughter to bear a love child out of wedlock. The pressures of survival that exist in different cultural contexts are thus brought to bear upon the absence of options and choice, by focussing on the poet's inchoate feelings and uncannily accurate analysis of real life situations. Hence, when the poet makes a bold declaration of independence saying:

I am seriously thinking of disowning you, Papa
You and your sacredness

the profession remains a thought that cannot be translated into action and sounds more convincing as the articulation of wish fulfillment rather than intentional defiance. Also, Mamta Kalia's own near-conventional life-style supports this contention even though her poems may reflect a "rebellion against patriarchy" as William Walsh suggests (155), that leaves little or no room for choice. The poet however, does not advocate promiscuity either through the covert suggestion of sexual freedom or the irrationality of the female virginity myth as it exists in the male psyche. This is a theme Kalia had explored even in her first novel *Beghar* (Homeless). Inordinate and unconscious deference to the desires and designs of the patriarchal will however, courts a different kind of loneliness that brings in its wake a sense of either being adrift, hemmed in or obliterated, says the poet:

I don't know how it has happened
but the road seems narrower without you . . . .
In reality

all our friends were your friends,
all our ideas your ideas
all our projects your projects.
I followed you like a corollary. (23)

Again, contrary to Chavan's argument that the poet's sensibility "is almost exclusively subjective in response to experience" (72), Kalia's poetry reflects a keen social consciousness and is far from a maudlin, private lament. She assigns the poet a role of social responsibility and sees poetry as its own form of activism even though writing may take "a hundred years to create a ripple" (*TP* 60). Admitting that poetry may not be able to affect immediate change, she lives on in the hope of being able to alter perception if and when she is heard and read. As she tells de Souza, "On the threshold of a brand new century, who knows, people may just tire of telly inanities, electronic amenities, information bonanzas, and get back to books" (64). For her art is an armor, a defense against the pressures of a chaotic reality. Although there is a dichotomy between artistic impulse and conscious action, there is never any doubt about the honesty of intent. What follows is a finely controlled acceptance of the necessity for constant adjustments to our perception, of what can be admitted to the category of accepted behavior and community sensibility. Far from being iconoclastic, Mamta Kalia's poetry reflects a recognition and appreciation of the fact that individual sensibilities will inevitably be influenced in the expression of a renewed sense of identity and self-value, by the literary, aesthetic and societal assumptions of their own culture. Hence the "relaxed attitude to poetry" that de Souza appreciates (*EDS* 18) and the scaled-down persona that preserves so much of the import, purpose and effect of her work. Her poems move neither "towards anarchy," nor "nihilism" as her friends and readers allege (*TP* 59). They record no acrimonious and belabored debates on relational and personal conflicts, but give a perfectly controlled account of their engagement with social concerns, in open-ended forms that encourage audience participation.

Mamta Kalia is no strident, feminist activist either. Yet her poetry shares a vital concern with the basic proposition of women's demands for an equitable life. Like Nora put it in Ibsen's *A Doll's House*, more than a century ago: "Before everything else I am a human being." That she does not conform to the Barbie doll image and protests against the treatment of women as sex objects, is quite evident from the unconventional, de-romanticized, de-glamorized self-portrait that she presents:

in an ill-fitting kurta,
a fag and minus-four glasses. (22)

Also, supporting the feminist agenda for liberation from patriarchal oppression, is her critical cataloguing of the several harrowing possibilities that retrogressive practices violative of human dignity, could expose women to. Female fate seems to hang precariously in a balance that could tilt over any moment:

I could have been kidnapped
at the age of seven
and ravaged by
dirty-minded middle-aged men.
I could have been married off
to a man with a bad smell
and turned frigid. . . . .
I could have been
an illiterate woman
putting thumb-prints
on rent receipts.
But nothing ever happened to me
except two children
and two miscarriages. (21)

The poem strategically but forcefully conveys through a dissimulating flippancy and lightness of touch, the underlying poignancy of women who have no control either over their fates or their bodies. It underscores the enormity of physical and psychological abuse, both within and outside institutionalized and socially sanctioned gender relationships. This recalls Adrienne

Rich's inference that healthy heterosexual relationships are not normative, but more a matter of chance. It is no accident then, that the poet has significantly entitled her poem 'Sheer Good Luck.' The related issue of conjugal harmony and its many intricate ramifications is taken up in yet another poem 'After Eight Years of Marriage' (25-26):

> After eight years of marriage
> The first time I visited my parents,
> They asked, 'Are you happy, tell us?'
> It was an absurd question
> And I should have laughed at it.
> Instead, I cried.
> And in between sobs, nodded yes.

This poem too, is a sad commentary on community attitudes and customs that enforce a fictional happiness on men and women to escape the stigma and attendant responsibilities of broken marriages. Cribbed, confined and consigned, people drag themselves through a lifetime of bickering and friction that is the natural outcome of soured and incompatible relationships. "Instead of post-modernism we should be talking about post barbarism" the poet says indignantly (*TP* 60). Neither hysterical nor militant, Kalia demands discourse and dialogue, not protests and marches, for possible solutions.

Mamta Kalia's poetry in English is yet to receive the critical acclaim or attention that it deserves. This does not however undermine its worth and purpose, which is a demand for a greater consideration of and attention to the problems inherent in our day to day reality. Poetic strength comes from her ability to maintain a fine tension between the private and the public. She comes across as a quiet, confident woman with a sound head on her responsible shoulders and her feet planted firmly on the ground. In the midst of an unpromising present in which, intrinsic worth falls prey to material considerations, her sardonic wit and irony help restore equipoise. No fiery monster out to wreak vengeance, her poetic persona is not the alienated and isolated self of Western literature, but a level-headed woman in touch with her community. Without being openly defiant she can hold her own and is part of her society, towards which she acknowledges a few explicit obligations and commitments. Mamta Kalia's art is thus a symbiosis of the personal and the social.

Works Cited

Chavan, Sunanda P. 1984. *The Fair Voice: A Study of Indian Women Poets in English.* New Delhi: Sterling.

_________. "Modern Indian English Women Poets: An Overview." *Perspectives on Indian Poetry in English.* M.K. Naik, ed. 1984. New Delhi: Abhinav Publications. 190-207.

de Souza, Eunice. 1999. *Talking Poems: Conversations with Poets.* New Delhi: Oxford University Press.

__________. Ed. 1997. *Nine Indian Women Poets: An Anthology.* New Delhi: OUP.

Iyengar, K.R.S. 1999. *Indian Writing in English*. New Delhi: Sterling.

Kalia, Mamta. *Nine Indian Women Poets.* Ed. Eunice de Souza. 1997. New Delhi: Oxford University Press. Hereafter cited as *EDS.*

Walsh, William. 1990. *Indian Literature in English.* London and New York: Longman.

Afterword

As far back as 1821, Shelley had declared in his *Defence of Poetry,* that poets are the unacknowledged legislators of the world. Almost sixty years later Mathew Arnold, affected by the *mal du siecle* expressed by other European writers had in *The Study of Poetry*, expressed the view that: "most of what now passes with us for religion and philosophy will be replaced by poetry." More than a century later Adrienne Rich has reiterated: "poetry is potentially catalytic speech." In our violent and disintegrative times the question that is often asked is, can poetry make a 'difference'? Can it persist, she wonders, "as a ligative art rather than as an echo chamber of fragmentation and alienation"? Although not much of the romantic idea of the poet as an exalted figure and poetry as the expression of elevated thoughts and feelings remains in modern notions of poet and poetry, the idea is still discernible in the response of a sizable section of the population, to the arts. Poetry is being commoditized and more and more people are reading and believing in its efficacy. When fashion in twentieth century literature turned against the more extravagant claims for the poet and his art inherited from the Romantic Movement, authors of poems were given a neutral context by being referred to as 'practitioners' of 'verse' and not 'poets' writing 'poetry.' This was especially evident in the writings of F.R. Leavis and the *Scrutiny* group as also in the works of many other critics in the 1930s, 1940s, and 1950s. Leavis' demand for more rigorous intellectual standards had led to his iconoclastic attacks on Spenser, Milton and Shelley, even while he traced the main line of English poetry through Donne, Pope, and Dr. Johnson to Hopkins, Eliot and, with some reservations, Yeats. Although Leavis had radically altered the literary map of the past, giving them a neutral context could not neutralize the words 'poet' and 'poetry' and there is still a curious power that resides in the idea of poetry.

If language represents power in society, poetry has been generally conceded to the most comprehensive use of language. Language is the presence of the community and the community and its poetry are not two. Populations are still influenced and ultimately controlled by the word and though the poet is no longer rhetorician and public bard, the sense that he has a better understanding of that source of power earns a deference, which is real. Albeit in this age of specialization when other sciences have their own languages, the function of poetry has contracted, yet it too has become more specialized, more arcane, more mysterious in spirit. What distinguishes the language of poetry from other languages however, is that while other specialized languages have a specific function to perform, the purpose of poetry is to survive any particular use and is comprehensive enough to attain a life of its own beyond any specific purpose. Nevertheless, poetry is denied autonomy of identity on account of meaningless and acrimonious arguments between aesthetes and moralists about the proper aim and objective of poetry, when the intention is to answer one another rather than look at the object of dispute, which lies between them. Likewise, modern literary theorists have denied the existence of the innocent reader, which to an extent is arguably true. Nonetheless, beneath our special interests and ideological or theoretical commitments are those human qualities, which are general and are the innocent ground of our humanity. And, as Wordsworth has justly stated in his *Preface to the Lyrical Ballads*, the reader of poetry should be addressed "not as a lawyer, a physician, a mariner, an astronomer, or a neutral philosopher but as a Man." It is to this 'Man,' that is the common reader in every specialist, that poetry addresses itself.

Again, what distinguishes a poem from prose is not form but the quality of intensity, force, density, and luminosity. So heightened and powerful is the effect of poetic language that one feels exalted as in the presence of beautiful things. Whether in prose or metric form, language that is heightened and powerful in effect and in which, words have a greater life and energy than just meaning, is poetry. There is openness, a suggestiveness that is responsible for some of the best effects of poetry, for poems can mean many different things to different readers. There is such a complex potential in the operations of language that it is almost impossible to be simultaneously conscious of all the things a rich poetic text is doing at any one moment. Through its very being, it expresses meanings beyond the words it is contained in. The poet achieves this through a kind of speeding up of the mental process or what poets have traditionally called inspiration. Though not all poetry is inspired and poets have often crafted their poems through many painful drafts, it must be conceded that poetry is a highly personal art, which is the collaborative effort of invention and the higher faculty of imagination. It represents man's highest intellectual and spiritual achievements even while it pleases, enlightens and exalts through superior entertainment.

Current critical theory, however, has made attempts to deprive poets and poetry of the power that was hitherto ascribed to them by insisting that the poet is irrelevant, even non-existent and that there is no 'poem' but a 'text.' In his essay, 'The Death of the Author,' Roland Barthes had asserted the primacy of the reader in the creation of a text negating all efforts of the writer as author of a text. This, however, has been one of the most controversial tenets of post-structuralism. Barthes' contention, like that of several other critics is, that when the 'text' is read by the reader, the poem comes into being, uniquely. The multiplicity of the text is focused in the reader and not as was hitherto believed, in the author. The critic has thus written himself into a position of primacy so that the significant creative skill passes from the poet to the reader and is demonstrated in what the critic makes of the text. Poetry however, is so intrinsic an upshot of linguistic life and consciousness, that it will survive in one form or the other despite the debates about the nature and the function of poetry. As Adrienne Rich states in a recent online interview with Paulo da Costa: "poetry has always mattered, through human history, through all kinds of cultures, all kinds of violence and human desolation, as well as periods of affirmation. It has been associated with the power of the word, with the sacred, with magic and transformation, with the oral narratives, words, speech, voice, breath, music, bodily tempo and its powers of the imagination."

The noted critic Helen Vendler too believes, that lyric poetry neither stands nor falls on its themes but on "the accuracy of language with which it reports the author's emotional responses to the life around him." In the pursuit of current literary fashion then, a poet must not lose trust in his own poetic possibilities and must attempt to preserve an awareness of his own poetic process and faith in the possibility of his poetry. In this context, whatever the poets in the preceding chapters may have lacked, they possess and nourish this faith in their own creative instincts and believe that ideally, poetry can have practical, psychological, social and spiritual benefits. Poets are in a constant state of what Rich terms as "cognitive dissonance," and believe that justice and creativity has something intrinsically in common. Art has the power to draw us out of ourselves, activate psychic energies, motivate decisions and empower actions that lead to the achievement of practical goals. Unlike Auden who believed that poetry does nothing, these poets share a faith in the power of symbolic action, through its ability to alter the basic structures of emotion. Once they have found the symbolic plane on which to sketch a topic, they have endeavored consciously and constantly, to find a way to prolong that symbolic plane through time.

The idea of studying a body of lyric poetry as a series of developmental stages is to heighten our aesthetic appreciation of the subtle and sudden changes in the arc of the poet's development and to discover in the process, the uniqueness of his or her contribution. Each successful poem presents itself as a unique experiment in language and indicates the provisional nature of all lyric compositions, which deal with the poet's consciousness at a given point of time. Each, as Keats said in an 1818 letter to his publisher John Taylor, is "a regular stepping of the Imagination towards a Truth" (Letters 59), since no lyric can be equal to the whole complexity of private and public life at any given moment. Lyrics therefore are not to be read as position papers. Deeply engaged with the problem of self-portraiture and self-definition, the poets in the preceding chapters are stubborn in their belief in the incalculable power of poetry to help us go on. Whether or not the reconstructions of thought that their poems embody can lead to our survival is debatable, but without such reconstruction we will remain mired in our present inadequate modes of thinking. As Rich says: "art is both tough and fragile. It speaks of what we long to hear and what we dread to find. Its source and native life, the imagination, may be shackled in early life yet may find release in conditions offering little else to the spirit." The artist, who in the role of responsible citizen challenges institutionalized power, has recognized the inseparability of art from acute social crisis. Literary texts are therefore, crucial to the formation of ideological discourse precisely because they work on the imagination and upon people as individuals. Poets may feel bitter about how little their work can do in the face of seemingly out-of-control technological power and limitless greed, yet the work of these poets stands testimony to the power of poetry to break isolation. It shows us to ourselves when we are belittled, dwarfed and excluded and reminds us of grace and kinship when all is represented as violence and separation. It can work out a connectedness with other people who are suffering, besieged and disenfranchised. Quoting John Berger, Rich infers with him that poetry can "repair no loss, but it defies the space that separates . . . by its continual labor of reassembling what has been scattered ." A similar idea finds echo in Muriel Rukeyser's belief that poetry can offer: "the truths of outrage and the truths of possibility." And this keeps alive our faith in the power of poetry, to restore some sense of order in our lives.

Bibliography

Abraham, Abu. "Kamala Surayya." *The Tribune.* January 2, 2000.

Aird, E.M. 1973. *Sylvia Plath: Her Life and Her Work.* New York: Barnes and Noble.

Alcoff, Linda. "Cultural feminism versus post-structuralism: the identity crisis in feminist theory." *Feminist Theory in Practice and Process.* Micheline R., Malson, et. al. Eds. 1989. Chicago and London: Univ. of Chicago Press. 295-332.

Atwood, Margaret. "Introduction." *The Paris Review Interviews: Women Writers at Work.* George Plimpton Ed. 1999. London: The Harville Press. VIII-XVIII.

Baig, Tara Ali. 1974. *Sarojini Naidu.* New Delhi: Sterling Publishers Pvt. Ltd.

Barry, Peter. 1995. *Beginning Theory.* Manchester: University Press.

Bennett, Paula. 1986. *My Life a Loaded Gun: Female Creativity and Feminist Poetics.* Boston: Beacon Press.

Bianchi, Martha. 1932. *Emily Dickinson Face to Face: Unpublished Letters with Notes and Reminiscences.* Boston and New York: Houghton Mifflin.

Bloom, Harold. "Poetic Origins and Final Phases." *Modern Criticism and Theory: A Reader.* David Lodge. Ed. 1992. New York: Longman.

Blos, Peter. 1962. *On Adolescence: A Psychoanalytical Interpretation.* New York: The Free Press of Glencoe.

Bullfinch, Thomas. 1993. *The Golden Age of Myth and Legend.* Hertfordshire: Wordsworth.

Chavan, Sunanda P. 1984. *The Fair Voice: A Study of Indian Women Poets in English.* New Delhi: Sterling.

______. "Modern Indian English Women Poets: An Overview." *Perspectives on Indian Poetry in English.* M.K. Naik. Ed. 1984. New Delhi: Abhinav.

Chodorow, Nancy. 1978. *The Reproduction of Mothering: Psychoanalysis and the Sociology of Gender.* Berkley: The University of California Press.

Cody, John. 1971. *After Great Pain: The Inner Life of Emily Dickinson.* Cambridge, Massachusetts: Harvard Univ. Press.

Cousins, James H. 1918. *The Renaissance of India.* Madras: Ganesh.

da Costa, Paulo. "Interview with Adrienne Rich." *Samsara Quarterly,* 2001. Downloaded from www.english.uiuc.edu/maps/poets/m_r/rich/onlineints.htm

Das, Kamala. 1996. *Only the Soul Knows How to Sing.* New Delhi: DD.

______. 1984. *Collected Poems.* Trivandrum: Navkerala.

______. 1975. *My Story.* New Delhi: Sterling.

______. 1973. *The Old Playhouse and Other Poems.* Calcutta: Writers' Workshop.

______. 1967. *The Descendants.* Calcutta: Writers' Workshop.

______.1965. *Summer in Calcutta.* Calcutta: Writers' Workshop.

de Souza, E. 1999. *Talking Poems: Conversations with Poets.* New Delhi: Oxford University Press.

______. Ed. 1997. *Nine Indian Poets: An Anthology.* New Delhi: Oxford University Press.

Dickinson, Emily. *The Complete Poems.* Thomas H. Johnson. Ed. 1960. Boston: Little Brown Press.

______. *Selected Letters.* Thomas H. Johnson. Ed. 1971. Cambridge Massachusetts: The Belknap Press of Harvard University.

Diehl, Joan Feit. "'Cartographies of Silence': Rich's Common Language and the Woman Poet." *Feminist Studies.* Fall 1980.

Dobson, Joanne A. "Oh, Suzie, it is Dangerous: Emily Dickinson and the Archetype." *Feminist Critics Read Emily Dickinson.* 80-85.

Du Plessis, Rachael Blau. 1986. *Hilda Doolittle: The Career of that Struggle.* Brighton: Harvester Press.

______. 1985. *Writing Beyond the Ending: Narrative Strategies of Twentieth Century Woman Writers.* Bloomington: Indiana Univ. Press.

Dwivedi, A.N. 1978. *Indo-Anglian Poetry.* Allahabad: Kitab Mahal.

______. 1992. *Sarojini Naidu and Her Poetry.* Allahabad: Kitab Mahal.

Evans, Judith. 1995. *An Introduction to Second-Wave Feminism.* London: Sage.

Faludi, Susan. 1992. *Backlash: The Undeclared War against American Women.* New York: Anchor/ Doubleday.

Fenton, James. "A Family Romance: *Birthday Letters*." *The New York Review.* March 5,1998. 7-9.

Flax, Jane. "Postmodernism and gender relations in feminist theory." *Feminism/Postmodernism.* Linda Nicholson. Ed. 1990. London: Routledge. 39-62.

Friedan, Betty. 1974. *The Feminine Mystique.* New York: W.W. Norton.

Gary, Paul. "Breaking the Silence" *Time*. March 2, 1998. Vol. 151, no. 9.

Gelpi, Barbara and Albert. Ed. 1975. *Adrienne Rich's Poetry.* New York: W.W. Norton.

Gery, John. 1996. *Ways of Nothingness: Nuclear Annihilation and Contemporary American Poetry.* Florida: Board of Regents.

Gilbert, Sandra. "The Wayward Nun Beneath the Hill: Emily Dickinson and the Mysteries of Womanhood." *Feminist Critics Read Emily Dickinson.* Susan Juhasz. Ed. 1983. Bloomington: Indiana Univ. Press.

Gilbert, Sandra and Gubar, Susan. "Women Poets." *Literature in the Modern World: Critical Essays and Documents.* Denis Walder. Ed. 1990. New Delhi: Oxford Univ. Press.

Gilligan, Carol. 1992. *In a Different Voice.* London: Harvard Univ. Press.

Gosse, Edmund. 1912. "Introduction." *The Bird of Time: Songs of Life, Death and the Spring.* London: Heinemann.

Greer, Germaine. 1970. *The Female Eunuch.* New York: McGraw-Hill.

Harikrishnan, Charmy. "High Priestess of Love." *The Week.* December 26,1999.

Harish, Ranjana. "In the Cultural Hall of Mirrors: Issue of Gender, Genre Incompatibility in Women's Autobiography." *The Literary Criterion.* Vol. XXXL, no.182. 1996. 25-32.

Hughes, Ted. 1998. *Birthday Letters.* New York: Farrar, Straus and Giroux.

_______. Ed. 1981. *Sylvia Plath: Collected Poems.* London: Faber and Faber.

Iyengar, K.R.S. 1999. *Indian Writing in English.* New Delhi: Sterling.

Iype, George. "When the temptress dawns the *purdah.*" December14, 1999. Rediff on the net.

Jacobus, Mary. ""The Difference of View." *Women Writing and Writing about Women.* Jacobus. Ed. 1979. New York: Barnes and Noble.

Jain, Jasbir. Ed. 2000. *Creating Theory: Writers on Writing.* Delhi: Pencraft International.

Jong, Erica. "Visionary Anger." *Adrienne Rich's Poetry*. Barbara and Albert Gelpi. Ed. 1975. New York: W.W. Norton.

Juhasz, Susan. Ed. 1983. *Feminist Critics Read Emily Dickinson.* Bloomington: Indiana Univ. Press

Jung, Anees. "From Kamala to Suraiya: As Faith Decrees." *The Tribune*, February 16, 2003.

Jussawala, Adil. *Journal of Commonwealth Literature*. No. 5, 1968. 66.

Kakar, Sudhir. 1989. *Intimate Relations: Exploring Indian Sexuality.* New Delhi: Viking.

Kalia, Mamta 1978. *Poems '78*. Calcutta: Writers' Workshop.

______. 1970. *Tribute to Papa and Other Poems*. Calcutta: Writers' Workshop.

Kalinnikova, Elena J. 1982. *Indian English Literature*. Trans. V.P. Sharma. Ghaziabad: Vimal.

Kaur, Iqbal. 1995. *Perspectives on Kamala Das's Poetry.* New Delhi: Intellectual.

Keller, Karl. 1979. *The Only Kangaroo among the Beauty: Emily Dickinson and America.* Baltimore and London: The John Hopkins Univ. Press.

Keyes, Claire. 1986. *The Aesthetics of Power: The Poetry of Adrienne Rich.* Athens: The Univ. of Georgia.

Khan, Izzat Yaar. 1983. *Sarojini Naidu: The Poet.* New Delhi: S. Chand.

King, Bruce. Ed. 1992. *Modern Indian Poetry.* New Delhi: Oxford Univ. Press.

Klein, Michael. "A Rich Life: Adrienne Rich on Poetry, Politics and Personal Revelation." *The Boston Phoenix*. June 1999.

Kolodny, Annette. "Feminist Literary Criticism." *Critical Enquiry,* Autumn 1975. 75-92.

______. "Inventing a Feminist Discourse: Rhetoric and Resistance in Margaret Fuller's *Woman in the Nineteenth Century." New Literary History: A Journal of Theory and Interpretation.* Vol. 25, no. 2. Spring 1994. 355-82.

Kroll, Judith. 1976. *Chapters in a Mythology: the Poetry of Sylvia Plath.* New York: Harper and Row.

Kukil, Karen V., ed. 2000. *The Unabridged Journals of Sylvia Plath.* New York: Anchor.

Leyda, Jay. 1960. *The Years and Hours of Emily Dickinson.* 2 vols. New Haven: Yale Univ. Press.

Lodge, David. Ed. 1988. *Modern Criticism and Theory: A Reader.* New York: Longman.

Lorde, Audre. 1984. "Poetry is not a Luxury." *Sister Outsider: Essays, and Speeches.* Trumansburg, New York: Crossing Press.

Maini, D.S. 1998. *The Spirit of American Literature.* New Delhi: Sterling.

Martin, Wendy. 1984. *An American Triptych: Anne Bradstreet, Emily Dickinson and Adrienne Rich.* Chapel Hill and London: The Univ. of North Carolina Press.

______. "From Patriarchy to the Female Principle." *Adrienne Rich's Poetry.* Barbara and Albert Gelpi. Ed. 172-89.

Maso, Carole. "The Sylvia Lining." *The Village Voice Literary Supplement.* Oct.-Nov. 2000.

Mckay, D.F. "Aspects of Energy in the Poetry of Dylan Thomas and Sylvia Plath." *The Critical Quarterly.* Vol. 16, no. 1. Spring 1974. 53-67.

Mehrotra, A.K. Ed. 1990. *Twenty Indian Poems.* New Delhi: Oxford Univ. Press.

Menon, Leela. "The Freedom and Bondage of Madhavikkutty." *The Indian Express.* December 19,1999.

Miller, Karl. "Ed in American Ego." *Times Literary Supplement.* February 6,1998. 7-9.

Mishra, L.N. 1995. *The Poetry of Sarojini Naidu.* Delhi: B.R.

Mitchell, Juliet. "Femininity, narrative and psychoanalysis." *Modern Criticism and Theory.* Ed. David Lodge. 425-30.

Mohanty, N. "A Feminist Perspective on Kamala Das's Poetry." *Perspectives on Kamala Das's Poetry.* Ed. Iqbal Kaur. 45-66.

Moyers, Bill. 1995. "Conversations with Adrienne Rich." *The Language of Life: A Festival of Poets.* New York: Doubleday. 335-53.

Nabar, Vrinda. 1994. *The Endless Female Hungers.* New Delhi: Sterling.

Naidu. Sarojini. 1961. *The Feather of the Dawn.* Padmaja Naidu. Ed. Bombay: Asia.

______. 1937. *The Sceptred Flute: Songs of India.* New York: Dodd, Mead.

______. 1930. *Selected Poems.* H.G. Dalway Turnbull. Calcutta: Oxford Univ. Press

______. 1917. *The Broken Wing: Songs of Love, Death and Destiny.* London: Heinemann

______. 1912. *The Bird of Time: Songs of Life, Death and Spring.* Intro. Edmund Gosse. London: Heinemann

______. 1905. *The Golden Threshold.* Intro. Arthur Symons. London: Heinemann

______. 1896. *Songs* by Miss S. Chattopadhyaya. Hyderabad: for private circulation.

______. 1893. *Mehir Muneer: A Poem in Three Cantos by a Brahmin Girl.* Madras: Shrinivasa, Vardachari.

Naik, M.K. Ed. 1984. *Perspectives on Indian Poetry in English.* New Delhi: Abhinav.

______. 1984. *Dimensions of English Literature.* New Delhi: Sterling.

Narasimhaiah, C.D. Ed. 1990. *An Anthology of Commonwealth Poetry.* Madras: Macmillan India.

Nelson, Cary. 1981. *Our Last First Poets: Vision and History in Contemporary American Poetry.* Urbana: Univ. of Illinois Press.

Oates, Jyoce Carol. "The Death Throes of Romanticism: The Poetry of Sylvia Plath." *Southern Review.* Vol. 9, no. 3. July 1973. Article revised on Nov. 16,1999. Downloaded from www.usfca.edu/facstaff/southerr/throes.html

Ossoli, Margaret Fuller. 1971. *Woman in the Nineteenth Century and Kindred Papers.* New York: W.W. Norton.

Paranjape, Makarand. Ed. 1984. *Sarojini Naidu: Selected Poetry and Prose.* New Delhi: Indus.

Parthasarthy, R. Ed. 2000. *Ten Twentieth Century Poets.* New Delhi: Oxford Univ. Press.

Pathiyan, Priya. "Interview with Kamala Das." *The Times of India Sunday Review.* April 1, 2001.

______. "We Love Kamala Das Because." *The Times of India Sunday Review.* March 2, 2003.

Plath, Aurelia. Ed. 1976. *Sylvia Plath: Letters Home.* London: Faber and Faber.

Plath, Sylvia. 2000. *The Unabridged Journals.* Karen V. Kukil. Ed. New York: Anchor.

______. 1983. *Journals*. Ted Hughes and Francis McCllough, ed. New York: Ballantine.

______. 1981. *Collected Poems.* Ted Hughes. Ed. London: Faber and Faber.

______. 1979. *Johnny Panic and the Bible of Dreams*. London: Faber and Faber.

______. 1976. *Letters Home.* Aurelia Plath. Ed. London: Faber and Faber.

______. 1966. *The Bell Jar*. London: Faber and Faber.

Plimpton, George. Ed. 1999. *The Paris Review Interviews: Women Writers at Work.* London: The Harville Press.

Pope, Deborah. 1995. "Rich's Life and Career." *The Oxford Companion to Women's Writing in the United States.* New York: Oxford University Press.

Prabha, M. 2000. *The Waffle of the Toffs: A Sociocultural Critique of Indian Writing in English.* New Delhi: Oxford and IBH.

Prince, Ruth E. C. "The Possibilities of an Engaged Art: An Interview with Adrienne Rich." *Radcliffe Quarterly*. Fall 1998.

Radicalesbians. "The Woman Identified Woman." *The Vintage Book of Feminism*. Ed. Miriam Schneir. 160-67.

Rajan, P.K. Ed. 1995. *Changing Traditions in Indian English Literature.* New Delhi: Creative.

Rajani, P. 2000. *The Poetry of Sylvia Plath.* Hyderabad: Orient Longman.

Raveendran, P.P. "Kamala Das: The Ideology of Intimacy." *Changing Traditions in Indian English Literature.* Ed. P.K. Rajan.

Rich, Adrienne. 2001. *Fox: Poems 1998-2000.* New York: W.W. Norton.

______. 2001. *Arts of the Possible: Essays and Conversations*. New York: W.W. Norton.

______. "Credo of a Passionate Skeptic." *Los Angeles Times*, March 11, 2001.

______. 1999. *Midnight Salvage: Poems 1995-1998*. New York: W.W. Norton.

______. 1995. *Dark Fields of the Republic: Poems 1991-1995.*

______. "Why I Refused the National Medal for the Arts." *Los Angeles Times Book Section*. August 3,1997.

______. Letter to Jane Alexander, Head, The National Endowment for the Arts. June 3, 1997. Downloaded from www.english.uiuc.edu/maps/poets/m_r/rich/onlineessays.htm

______. "Defy the Space That Separates." *The Nation*, October 7, 1996.

______. 1993. *Collected Early Poems.* New York: W.W. Norton.

______. 1993. *What is Found There: Notebooks on Poetry and Politics.* New York: W.W. Norton.

______. 1991. *An Atlas of the Difficult World: Poems 1988-1991.* New York: W.W. Norton.

______. 1986. *Your Native Land Your Life: Poems.* New York: W.W. Norton.

______. 1986. *Blood, Bread and Poetry: Selected Prose 1975-1985.* New York: W.W. Norton.

______. 1984. *The Fact of a Doorframe: Poems Selected and New 1950-1984.* New York: W.W. Norton.

______. 1981. *A Wild Patience Has Taken Me This Far: Poems 1978-1981.* New York: W.W. Norton.

______. 1979. *On Lies Secrets and Silence: Selected Prose 1966-1978.* New York: W.W. Norton.

______. 1978. *The Dream of a Common Language: Poems 1974-1977.* New York: W.W. Norton.

______. 1976. *Of Woman Born: Motherhood as Experience and Institution.* New York: W.W. Norton.

______. 1973. *Diving into the Wreck: Poems 1971-1972.* New York: W.W. Norton.

______. 1973. *The Will to Change: Poems 1968-1970.* New York: W.W. Norton.

______. 1972. *Leaflets: Poems 1965-1968.* New York: W.W. Norton.

______. 1966. *Necessities of Life: Poems 1962-1965.* New York: W.W. Norton.

______. 1963. *Snapshots of a Daughter-in-Law: Poems 1954-1962.* New York: W.W. Norton.

______. 1951. *A Change of World.* New Haven: Yale Univ. Press.

Rothschild, Mathew. "Adrienne Rich: I happen to think poetry makes a huge difference." *The Progressive,* 1994. Downloaded from www.english.uiuc.edu/maps/poets/m_r/rich/progressive.htm

Sagar, Keith. 2000. *The Laughter of the Foxes: A Study of Ted Hughes.* Liverpool: Liverpool Univ. Press.

Schneir, Miriam. Ed. 1995. *The Vintage Book of Feminism: The Essential Writings of the Contemporary Women's Movement.* New York: Vintage.

Showalter, Elaine. "Feminist Criticism in the Wilderness." *Modern Criticism and Theory.* Ed. David Lodge.

Simpson, Pat. Marchand, Michele and Freeman, Anitra. "Adrienne Rich: Standing at the Intersection of Art and Activism." *Real Change News*. April 19, 2001.

Singh, Mina Surjit. "The Poetry of Adrienne Rich." *The Aligarh Journal of English Studies*. Vol. 19, no. 1. 1997.

______."The Confessional Voice of Kamala Das." *Perspectives on Kamala Das's Poetry.* Iqbal Kaur. Ed.

______. "Poetic Strategy in Emily Dickinson's 'My Life had stood-a Loaded Gun.'" *The Aligarh Journal of English Studies*. Vol. 22, no. 1. 2000.

Spender, Dale. 1985. *Man Made Language.* London: Routledge and Kegan Paul.

Steiner, Nancy. 1973. *A Closer Look at Ariel*. New York: Harper and Row.

Templeton, Alice. 1994. *The Dream and the Dialogue.* Knoxville: The Univ. Press.

Tonks, Rosemary. "Cutting the Marble." *New York Review of Books*. October 4,1973. 8-10.

Thwaite, Anthony. 1996. *Poetry Today: A Critical Guide to British Poetry 1960-1995*. London and New York: Longman.

Vendler, Helen. 1980. *Part of Nature, Part of the U.S.: Modern American Poetry.* Cambridge MA: Harvard Univ. Press.

Walsh, William. 1990. *Indian Writing in English*. London and New York: Longman.

Warrier, Shobha. "Interview with Kamala Das." 1996. Rediff on the net.

Werner, Craig. 1988. *Adrienne Rich: The Poet and her Critics*. Chicago: American Library Association.

Whicher, George. 1938. *This was a Poet: A Critical Biography of Emily Dickinson*. Ann Arbor: Univ. of Michigan Press.

Wilt, Judith. "Emily Dickinson: Playing House." *Boundary.* Winter 1984. Vol. 12, no. 2. 153-69.